Infant/Toddler Caregiving

A Guide to

Language Development and Communication

Second Edition

Edited by

Peter L. Mangione,
and Deborah Greenwald

Developed by
WestEd

for the
California Department of Education

  WestEd

Publishing Information

Infant/Toddler Caregiving: A Guide to Language Development and Communication (Second Edition) was developed by WestEd, San Francisco. See the Acknowledgments for the names of those who made significant contributions to this document.

This publication was edited by Faye Ong, working in cooperation with Peter L. Mangione and Deborah Greenwald, WestEd, and Tom Cole, Consultant, Child Development Division, California Department of Education. It was designed and prepared for printing by the staff of CDE Press, with the cover and interior design created and prepared by Juan Sanchez.

The document was published by the Department of Education, 1430 N Street, Sacramento, CA 95814. It was printed by the Office of State Publishing and distributed under the provisions of the Library Distribution Act and *Government Code* Section 11096.

ISBN 978-0-8011-1712-1

Ordering Information

Copies of this publication are available for purchase from the California Department of Education. For prices and ordering information, please visit the Department Web site at http://www.cde.ca.gov/re/pn/rc/ or call the CDE Press sales office at 1-800-995-4099; fax 916-323-0823. Mail orders must be accompanied by a check payable to California Department of Education, a purchase order, or a credit card number, including expiration date (Visa or MasterCard only). Purchase orders without checks are accepted from governmental agencies, educational institutions, and businesses. Telephone orders will be accepted toll-free (1-800-995-4099) for credit card purchases only.

Photo Credits

Sara Webb-Schmitz

Notice

The guidance in *Infant/Toddler Caregiving: A Guide to Language Development and Communication (Second Edition)* is not binding on local educational agencies or other entities. Except for the statutes, regulations, and court decisions that are referenced herein, this handbook is exemplary, and compliance with it is not mandatory. (See *Education Code* Section 33308.5.)

Prepared for printing
by CSEA members

Contents

A Message from the State Superintendent of Public Instruction

At the heart of who we are as human beings is our ability to communicate. Acquisition of language is one of the most important developmental accomplishments of early childhood. The ability to use language to communicate effectively has a profound impact on a young child's later success in school. Language skills also play an important role in establishing and maintaining positive relationships with family, peers, teachers, and other adults. As more and more families rely on care outside the home for their infants and toddlers, it is vital that we help teachers and providers understand how to support early language development and communication.

Beginning at birth, infants have an amazing capacity to communicate with the adults who care for them. Newborns prefer to look at the human face more than anything else. Watching a baby's face and eyes allows a teacher to detect the baby's interest in engaging in interaction and provides other important clues about the baby's needs. Sensitive reading of the baby's messages makes it possible to interact with individual children in ways that enhance their communicative competence and build the foundation for language development.

All infants and toddlers need rich experiences with language, both at home and in the child care environment. Support of the home language and culture occurs naturally when children are cared for by the family. However, when infants and toddlers are cared for outside the home, in environments where the language of the teacher or provider does not match that of the infant and family, thoughtful attention needs to be given to ensure the continuing development of the home language.

This guide has been written by noted experts in the field of early language development and communication. It is rich in practical guidelines and suggestions based on current theory, research, and evidence-based practices for infant care teachers and family home care providers. I believe the guidance in this publication will assist early care and education practitioners' efforts to enhance children's development and success in school and in life.

Tom Torlakson

TOM TORLAKSON
State Superintendent of Public Instruction

Acknowledgments

The second edition of this publication was developed by the Center for Child and Family Studies, WestEd, under the direction of J. Ronald Lally and Peter L. Mangione. Special thanks go to Jacqueline Sachs, Donna J. Thal, Kathleen McCartney, Wendy Wagner Robeson, Eugene E. García, Janet Gonzalez-Mena, and Peter L. Mangione for writing specific sections of this document; and to Tom Cole, Consultant, Child Development Division, California Department of Education, for reviewing the document and making recommendations on content.

Special thanks go to the following infant/toddler programs for allowing us to take photographs for this publication:

Associated Students Sacramento State University, Children's Center
Associated Students San Francisco State University, Children's Center
Chabot College Children's Program
Covina Child Development Center
Eben Ezer Family Child Care
King Family Child Care
Marin Head Start, 5th Avenue Early Head Start
Marin Head Start, Hamilton Campus
Marin Head Start, Indian Valley Campus
Marin Head Start, Meadow Park Campus
Presidio Child Development Center
Solano Community College Children's Programs
University of California Los Angeles, Infant Development Program
Yerba Buena Gardens Child Development Center

The second edition of this guide reflects much of the content of the first edition. In addition, it has been updated in several ways. All chapters have been reviewed and updated by the original authors to ensure that each chapter includes new information from research and up-to-date references. There is a new chapter on language development and literacy in the infant/toddler years. Resources have been updated, and California's recently published infant/toddler foundations on language development appear in the appendix.

Introduction

The following pages contain a wealth of information specifically written to help infant care teachers with their day-to-day efforts to support the language development and communication of infants and toddlers and their families. This guide, one of a series developed by the Program for Infant/Toddler Care (PITC), is a companion document to the PITC training institutes, trainer's manuals, and DVD series. The California Department of Education, in collaboration with WestEd, created the PITC—a research- and practice-based train-the-trainer series—to support infant care programs in providing quality care. The PITC addresses all the major caregiving domains, from providing a safe and healthy learning environment to establishing responsive relationships with families. *A Guide to Language Development and Communication* provides information related to Module III, Learning and Development, of the PITC training series.

The guide is divided into six sections written by nationally recognized experts. The first three sections address how infant care teachers can support early language development and communication in young, mobile, and older infants. Sections Four and Five consider the role of bilingualism and culture on the early development of language and communication. Section Six addresses early literacy experiences as infants and toddlers learn language.

Each of the first six sections focuses on either a particular developmental period or a special topic (bilingual development, culture, language development and literacy) in early language development and communication. Appendix A presents part of the *California Infant/Toddler Learning & Development Foundations* (California Department of Education 2009), which describe key areas of learning and development in the language development domain. The recommendations and practices presented in this guide support children's acquisition of knowledge and skills identified by the foundations. The guide underscores the importance of providing responsive, relationship-based care that is attentive to both the child's ongoing development and linguistic and cultural heritage. This approach to care provides an enriched, supportive environment for language development and communication based on close, respectful relationships with the child and the family members.

Section One:
The Young Infant

Introduction

*I*n this section, Jacqueline Sachs describes in detail the early language development of the young infant from birth to six months and the role of the caring adult in providing an environment supportive of language and communication needs. Jacqueline Sachs is Emeritus Professor of Communication Sciences at the University of Connecticut. She has written numerous papers on language development and taught courses on normal language acquisition to students in speech–language pathology and education. Among Dr. Sachs's interests is communication during the first year of life, which was the subject of a chapter she contributed to Jean Berko Gleason and Nan Bernstein-Ratner's textbook *The Development of Language.*

Emergence of Communication: Earliest Signs

Jacqueline Sachs

Between birth and six months of age, infants may seem completely helpless, but they are already communicating with caring adults in many fascinating ways. One of the first and most important abilities of infants is that of getting attention from adults. How babies are responded to and encouraged to communicate is very important for later language development. This chapter examines how infants perceive the world around them, what communicative messages they produce, and how infant/toddler care teachers can best interact with babies.

The Infant's Perceptual Abilities

Many people think newborns cannot see or hear. However, in addition to being able to feel, taste, and smell, a newborn can see and hear remarkably well.

Ability to See

Newborns see best at a distance of about 8 to 15 inches, the distance at which your face will be when you are feeding or playing with newborn infants. Babies look at what they like, and what they like best at birth is the human face. By watching the baby's face and eyes, you can tell whether the baby is interested in interacting or wants to be alone.

Ability to Hear

Even before birth, the fetus can hear sounds such as the mother's heartbeat and voice. At birth, infants prefer their mother's voice and the sounds of the language they have been exposed to over other sounds. However, newborns come well equipped to learn any language, since they can also hear all the sounds that would be used in other languages.

It is important that infants hear lots of speech in the first year of life because, in the absence of speech sounds, the brain areas for the perception of speech do not develop normally (Kuhl 2004). By one year of age, babies begin to lose the ability to discriminate sounds they do not hear in the language spoken around them. For example, in a study of babies who were exposed only to English, infants between six and eight months of age could discriminate sounds used in Hindi or Salish. By ten to twelve months of age, that ability began to disappear (Werker and Tees 1984). The period before a baby says the first word was once called the "prelinguistic period." We now know that important language learning is taking place throughout the first year of life.

Communicative Messages

Nature has equipped infants with two major strategies to get the adult's attention. The first is crying. Because cries are noisy and generally unpleasant to listen to, we are motivated to figure out what is wrong so the infant will stop crying. Second, infants are cute and do cute things, such as cooing, babbling, smiling and making funny faces. This cuteness draws us to infants and makes us want to interact with them.

Crying

Although crying in a young infant is not deliberate communication, it does serve as the first communicative message to the caring adult. Many experts suggest that by responding to the baby's cries, you allow the baby to learn at an early age that communication is possible and useful. The sounds made by the baby while crying become more differentiated as the infant gets older. As you get to know an individual baby, you may be able to interpret the cry as meaning "I'm hungry," "I'm hurting," or "I'm tired."

Cooing

These pleasant sounds (something like "oooo") are the earliest sounds made as a result of friendly social interaction. They often emerge at about two months of age, but there is considerable individual variation among babies. Infants are delighted when we talk or "oooo" back to them.

Babbling

Most infants begin babbling at about six months of age. Babbling indicates that the infants are experimenting with the feelings in their mouths and sounds of their voices. Babies babble both socially and when alone. Like unresponsiveness to speech sounds, the absence of babbling may be a warning sign, although babies vary considerably in how much they babble.

The presence of babbling is not a guarantee that a baby's hearing is normal, because even babies who are profoundly deaf begin to babble. However, their babbling usually starts somewhat later than that of hearing babies, and eventually babies who cannot hear stop babbling.

Therefore, it is important for teachers to pay careful attention if an infant's babbling stops. If that happens, they need to communicate with the family members about having the infant's hearing checked for potential hearing loss or inability to hear.

Babies who babble a lot may be perceived by their teachers as more fun to interact with, but it is important to keep in mind that quiet babies deserve just as much attention as the more vocal ones.

Nonverbal Communication

In addition to making sounds, the young infant communicates with the face and body. For example, smiling usually appears at about the same time as cooing—around two months of age. The baby's ever-changing facial expressions and body movements can indicate a great deal about the baby's needs and moods. These actions are part of the baby's communication at this early age.

As an infant/toddler care teacher, you should be aware that there are differences in the ways various cultural groups interact with young infants and that those differences may be reflected in the way the infant interacts with you. For example, some babies live in an environment with almost constant human contact; babies are held, cuddled, passed from person to person, and carried about (Heath 1983). In such a setting, a lot of nonverbal communication is part of the close physical contact between the baby and the caring adults. It would not be surprising if an infant from such a culture were to be distressed at not being held in a child care setting. The infant might have a rich repertoire of nonverbal communication, but this repertoire has developed in a specific cultural setting and might not be displayed when the setting is different. Two-way communication with family members can help you identify ways to interact that are familiar to the infant. Section Five,

"Culture and Communication," provides more information on cultural differences in infant care.

Interaction with Young Infants

It is important that the infant/toddler care teacher's interaction with an infant who is less than six months old be on a one-to-one basis, even though the infant is part of a group. It is crucial that each baby, not just the most demanding ones, get some undivided attention. There are two aspects to interaction: stimulating communication and responding to communicative attempts. Stimulation can be thought of as what you do on your own initiative, and your responsiveness is how you respond when the baby initiates an interaction.

Stimulating Communication

The first section, "The Infant's Perceptual Abilities," discussed the importance of infants hearing speech in the first year

of life. But one might ask, how much speech and what sort of speech? The answer depends on both the infant's current state and temperament.

Learn to recognize each infant's state and rhythm of transition from one state to another. All babies vary from time to time in how ready they are for interaction, depending on their current state: fully alert, awake but not alert, drowsy, or sleeping. During the fully alert state, the baby may look around, coo, smile, and make eye contact. These behaviors often mean the baby is ready to interact.

Babies also need rest and quiet times. Their state constantly changes, so you must be able to assess the infant's present state. You will know if the baby is not interested in play by signs such as looking away, fussing, or even falling asleep! But do not be too concerned about missing a cue and continuing to communicate with a child who may have lost interest or may need a rest. One expert on the interactional patterns of adults and infants has suggested that occasional "messing up" is potentially a stimulus for growth (Stern 2002). Infants learn that their trusted adults are responsive to them, but they also learn to cope when the adults occasionally respond in a way that does not match their current interest or need.

Considering the infant's temperament helps you decide whether and to what degree an interaction should be stimulating or soothing. For more information about temperament, refer to the article by Stella Chess in *Infant/Toddler Caregiving: A Guide to Social–Emotional Growth and Socialization, Second Edition* (California Department of Education 2011) and to the DVD *Flexible, Fearful, or Feisty: The Different Temperaments of Infants and Toddlers.* The "easy" infant may be able to handle highly stimulating interaction, whereas the "difficult" infant

may need a more soothing approach. The "slow-to-warm-up" infant may need to be approached first in a soothing way, but later the infant may respond happily to stimulating play. Again, however, beware of categorizing a baby by temperament type. These types exist on a continuum; for appropriate communicative interaction, you need to get to know each baby individually. Learn to recognize when to interact and what kind of stimulation brings out the best in each baby.

When infants are in a mood to interact, make sure to be attentive to them. This mutual attending is the beginning of communication, and later language development rests on establishing such patterns during the earlier stages. Do not provide only care; be a playmate as well. You may think it does not matter whether you talk to such young babies when they cannot understand your words, but the "music" of your voice is more important than the words.

Use baby talk. This recommendation may be a surprise because in our culture the term "baby talk" has some negative connotations. We think of it as saying only things like "tummy" for "stomach" or "choo-choo" for "train." Some people say they never use baby talk with young children. If you listen to those people, however, they certainly do not talk to an infant or young child in the same way they talk to an adult. If they did, they would not hold the child's attention for very long. I am using the term "baby talk" in its broader sense, that is, as speech modified to be interesting and understandable to young children. This sort of baby talk is indeed appropriate for a baby.

In the research literature, you may see baby talk referred to as "infant-directed speech." Special ways of speaking to infants and young children are found in all cultures and have similar features almost

everywhere. Baby talk has a generally higher pitch with more overall variation in pitch (some words very high and some very low), dramatic variations in loudness (even whispers often hold the baby's attention), and an exaggerated stress on words that forms a regular rhythmic pattern. Baby talk holds the infants' attention better than adult-to-adult speech does, even for two-day-old babies (Cooper and Aslin 1990).

Fortunately, you do not have to *learn* how to use baby talk. Adults have the ability to modify their language to interact appropriately with children at any stage of language learning. If one pays attention to the baby's reactions, baby talk will come quite naturally—especially if one does not worry about sounding silly to another adult.

An expressive face, as well as an expressive voice, helps the baby to be attentive. Exaggerated expressions, such as surprise or frowns, go along with baby talk. Eye contact is held much longer in interaction with infants than with adults. The primary reason for using baby talk, exaggerated facial expressions, and prolonged eye contact is that they hold the infant's attention and thus help you and the baby get to know each other as individuals.

The first messages you convey will be emotional ones. *What* you say does not matter, but *how* you say it and *what you really feel* when you say it do matter. When your emotions are not positive, your real feelings have a way of "showing" through in your voice and face. If you say, "You're my little sweetie pie," but you feel bored and irritable, the negative messages will probably be the ones that come through. Rather, you communicate best when you are not distant but emotionally involved with each baby.

One easy way to increase the amount of speech that an infant hears is simply to talk about what you are doing (self-talk). For example, you might say "Now I'm going to get your bottle." You can also talk about what you notice about the baby (parallel talk). For example, when the baby smiles, you comment, "Oh, what a big smile!"

Putting a young infant in front of a TV set, even one playing material supposedly designed for children, is not an effective way to increase the baby's exposure to language. It is tempting to use the TV as a babysitter, but research has shown that speech on TV is not a substitute for human interaction. Language learning takes place through social interaction (Kuhl, Tsao, and Liu 2003).

Responding to Communicative Attempts

In addition to providing stimulation, teachers should respond to the baby's initiations. Infants are social and want to communicate. By responding to the infant, you provide important lessons about communication from a very early age. Long before the first word is uttered, and even well before the first word is understood, the infant has learned a great deal about how language works. Adults are teaching three lessons in responding to infants.

Lesson 1: Communication matters. One of the first communicative lessons adults teach infants is, "People will pay attention to you when you try to communicate." Acknowledging the baby's subtle behavioral cues and bids for attention will help the baby learn this lesson.

When the baby smiles, coos, waves his or her hands, or otherwise tries to attract your attention, you probably respond naturally by nodding, smiling, or talking. By paying attention to the baby's social behavior much of the time, you help the infant learn about the world. Anything you do to let the baby know you have noticed the bid for attention, such as laughing, talking, smiling, or responding with an animated facial expression, helps that child feel important and loved.

Infants differ in how much they initiate interaction, so you need to keep in mind not to give less time to the relatively passive infant who does not demand attention. Do not worry about "spoiling" a young infant who is more demanding. You want to give all infants a sense that they can affect their environment.

Also keep in mind that the baby's focus of interest provides an opportunity to introduce language. If the baby is looking intently at a spoon, that is a good time to say "spoon." Here you use a "responsive interaction style"—following the child's focus of interest. In contrast, suddenly introducing a spoon into the situation and saying "spoon, spoon" would be an example of an "intrusive (or controlling) interactional style." Research has shown that infants benefit from responsive interaction (e.g., Baumwell, Tamis-Lemonda, and Bornstein 1997).

Some parents may use symbolic gestures, as well as words, in their interactions at home. Linda Acredolo and Susan Goodwyn (1996) published an influential book called *Baby Signs: How to Talk with Your Baby Before Your Baby Can Talk.* They suggested that infants could pick up gestures that are consistently paired with words for objects or actions, and that use of such gestures would provide an additional way for adults and young children to communicate. If the parents of a baby are using such signs, it is good for you to use them in a responsive interactional style, just as you do with words.

Lesson 2: People take turns communicating. The next lesson the infant learns is "Sometimes I talk and you listen; sometimes you talk and I listen." An infant first becomes aware of turn-taking when the adult *gives* the baby a turn. For example, Catherine Snow (1977) videotaped mothers interacting with babies three months of age. She found that the mothers left spaces in their vocalizations for the infants' turns and accepted anything they did (a smile, a coo, or even a burp!) as a conversational turn. The following interaction is one example of a "conversation" between a mother and her three-month-old daughter, Ann (Snow 1977, 12):

ANN: (Smiles)

MOTHER: "Oh, what a nice little smile! Yes, isn't that nice? There. There's a nice little smile."

ANN: (Burps)

MOTHER: "What a nice wind as well! Yes, that's better, isn't it? Yes. Yes. Yes!"

ANN: (Vocalizes)

MOTHER: "That's a nice noise."

What mothers accepted as turns changed over time. The mothers of older infants began to ignore things such as burps and to respond only to babblings as a turn.

Turn-taking is a good way to avoid overstimulating a young infant because you leave space for responses and can pay attention to those responses. You want the baby to learn to be an *active* conversational partner.

Lesson 3: Sounds are an important part of routines. Infants begin to learn the meaning of words through the repeated use of sounds or words in routines and rituals. Although most babies will not begin to speak until they are about a year old, they begin much earlier to expect certain sounds in certain contexts. To begin to break into the complex code that language is, babies need consistent pairings of sounds with objects and activities.

One source of these pairings is in baby games. Some standard games (for example, "peek-a-boo," "I'm gonna get you," and "give-and-take") are found many places in the world. Although the adult may think of these games as only play, infants learn by playing them.

Individual, invented games are just as important and useful in interacting with babies. Any playful thing you repeat can become a game with that baby. Even during the first six months of life, the baby will gradually learn what to expect in the game. The particular sounds or words in the games are not important—they may be "moo," for what the cow says, or "so big," in the game of "How big is baby?" or "boop," with a touch on the nose. What is happening is that the baby is being given the chance to realize that a sound goes with a situation.

Do not expect the six-month-old infant to be able to imitate these sounds or produce them spontaneously. Usually, signs that the baby has expectations about sounds in routine situations do not emerge until the second half of the first year. The first use of language typically emerges in these routine situations. By nine months of age, the baby will probably understand some words, and by a year, begin to speak. But the baby has been preparing for those steps from the beginning, during the important first six months of interaction with loving, responsive adults.

Reasons for Concern

Not being interested in social contact is a warning sign. For example, the baby who never looks in people's eyes when they attempt to make eye contact, or the baby who holds his body rigidly when in your arms, is not engaging in social interaction typical of young infants. (See appendix B, "Reasons for Concern That Your Child or a Child in Your Care May Need Special Help.")

Not attending to your speech is another sign. If a baby seems inattentive to the human voice, even when reactive to other loud noises, there is reason for concern. Speech sounds occur within a particular frequency range, and hearing within this range is necessary for normal language development. There are two possible reasons for inattention to the human voice:

1. If the baby does not seem to notice when people are talking to her, this may be a sign of a chronic hearing impairment. An assessment of the baby's hearing by an audiologist is possible even in the first six months of life. A hearing test is highly recommended if the baby seems unresponsive to speech; early intervention is possible and crucial for the child's normal language development.

2. Many babies develop ear infections or fluid in their ears because of respiratory infections. Sometimes it is obvious that something is wrong because the infant cries from the pain and may have a fever. Medical attention is necessary to combat the ear infection. However, many babies may seem to be well but nevertheless develop fluid in their ears that interferes with their hearing. Therefore, it is very important that teachers notice whether an infant responds normally when they speak. If a baby has become inattentive to speech, appropriate medical evaluation and intervention are imperative. Even temporary hearing problems caused by fluid in the ear, if they occur frequently, can have a long-term effect on language development.

Not beginning to coo or smile by three months of age and not beginning to babble by six months of age are other warning signs that warrant attention.

References

Acredolo, Linda, and Susan Goodwyn. 1996. *Baby Signs: How to Talk with Your Baby Before Your Baby Can Talk.* Chicago: Contemporary Books.

Baumwell, Lisa, Catherine S. Tamis-Lemonda, and Marc H. Bornstein. 1997. "Maternal Vocal Sensitivity and Child Language Comprehension," *Infant Behavior and Development* 20:247–58.

California Department of Education. 2009. *California Infant/Toddler Learning & Development Foundations.* Sacramento: California Department of Education.

———. 2011. *Infant/Toddler Caregiving: A Guide to Social-Emotional Growth and Socialization (Second Edition).* Sacramento: California Department of Education.

Cooper, Robin P., and Richard N. Aslin. 1990. "Preference for Infant-Directed Speech in the First Month After Birth," *Child Development* 61:1584–95.

Heath, Shirley B. 1983. *Ways with Words: Language, Life and Work in Communities and Classrooms.* New York: Cambridge University Press.

Kuhl, Patricia K. 2004. "Early Language Acquisition: Cracking the Speech Code," *Nature Reviews Neuroscience* 5:831–43.

Kuhl, Patricia K., F. Tsao, and H. Liu. 2003. "Foreign-Language Experience in Infancy: Effects of Short-Term Exposure and Social Interaction on Phonetic Learning," *Proceedings of the National Academy of Sciences, USA,* 100:9096–101.

Snow, Catherine. 1977. "The Development of Conversation between Mothers and Babies," *Journal of Child Language* 4:1–22.

Stark, Rachael E. 1986. "Prespeech Segmental Feature Development," in *Language Acquisition: Studies in First Language Development.* 2nd ed. Edited by Paul Fletcher and Michael Garman. New York: Cambridge University Press.

Stern, Daniel. 2002. *The First Relationship: Infant and Mother.* Rev. ed. Developing Child Series. Edited by Jerome Bruner and others. Cambridge, MA: Harvard University Press.

Werker, Janet, and Richard C. Tees. 1984. "Cross-language Speech Perception: Evidence for Perceptual Reorganization During the First Year of Life," *Infant Behavior and Development* 7:49–64.

Section Two:
The Mobile Infant

Introduction

In this section, Donna J. Thal describes the important milestones in the language development and communication of the mobile infant. She discusses in detail the concept of "joint reference" (when the baby and the caregiver focus on the same thing and start the first "conversation" about it). Dr. Thal explains how this early conversation supports the infant's developing language.

Donna J. Thal is Distinguished Professor Emerita of Speech and Hearing Sciences at San Diego State University and a research psychologist at the Center for Research and Language at the University of California at San Diego. The focus of Dr. Thal's research has been language and gestures in late talkers, continuity and variation in early language development in early childhood, and early identification of risk for specific language impairment. Dr. Thal has many years of clinical experience with children who have speech and language impairments.

Emergence of Communication: Give-and-Take Between Adult and Child

Donna J. Thal

In the previous section, Jacqueline Sachs showed that by six months of age, children have been involved in many important communicative exchanges. Young infants have learned that caring adults respond to their cries by providing the appropriate remedy (for example, a dry diaper, food, or a hug to make them feel secure). As a result, the infants have come to trust the adults who care for them. Because of this early experience, the children are ready for the next steps in the development of communication and language.

Language is the most important mental accomplishment of early childhood. Without the ability to use language skillfully, children are destined to fail in school, which makes them, as adults, less capable of competing successfully for good jobs. Without the ability to use language skillfully, children fail to establish positive relationships with peers and develop a pattern of isolation from social interaction. Thus, the development of language is a critical step in human growth. Between six and sixteen months of age, children take some of the most important steps in learning language, and it is vital that family members and infant/toddler care teachers recognize and reinforce these steps.

The purpose of this section is to help you learn to recognize how infants communicate and the changes in communication that occur in infants between six and sixteen months of age. Once you know what to expect, you will be able to interact with individual children in ways that will foster development of good language and communication.

Although you are responsible for more than one child at a time, remember that children this young cannot function as a group. At least at the beginning of this stage, infants are not aware of things much beyond their immediate reach. Part of the excitement of development in this age range is the infant's transition to mobility, which leads to exploration of larger spaces with more people and things. But the adult–child interactions that are most helpful to the child's development during this stage are still one-to-one.

Three important phenomena occur in the infant between six and sixteen months of age: (1) the establishment of joint reference to an object or activity with another person (usually an adult caregiver); (2) the onset of intentional communication; and (3) the use of conventional symbols (gestures, vocalizations, and words) to communicate with other people.

Establishment of Joint Reference— Six to Eight Months

By six months of age, the child has developed the physical and sensory distinctions of self and other. This awareness allows the child to master the first of the three phenomena described: establishing joint reference. *Joint reference* means that two people look at or pay attention to the same thing at the same time. The noted psychologist Daniel Stern described in detail how mothers and infants reach this point, emphasizing the back-and-forth, your turn–my turn type of interaction that mother and child practice from the early stages (Stern 1985, 2002). The establishment of joint reference is another step, along with the earlier turn-taking, in the "dance" of communication the child and adult have been developing. In a sense, joint reference is the first way that the topic of a "conversation" is established.

Awareness and Communication at Six Months

By six months of age, normal infants understand the turn-taking game, which they will continue to use in conversation when their language becomes more sophisticated. The infants also understand the rudiments of joint reference; they will observe the direction of the adult's gaze and then look in the same direction to find the object being looked at. Also by the time the infant is six months old, the adult and child have developed a number of cues by which they establish joint reference. While caring adults attend to an infant, they often look at objects and vocalize (that is, produce sounds such as "ooo" or words such as "look!") as well as change their intonation (such as raise the pitch of the voice).

Establishing joint attention goes in both directions. The six-month-old infant can follow the parent's line of sight, but parents also monitor the faces of the infants in their care and look at the objects and events to which the infants are attending. Usually, the parent also tries to determine exactly what has caught the infant's attention and provide a name for it. The most appropriate language-teaching strategies for infant care teachers to use are the same ones used by family members. Introducing words for what the infant is looking at or playing with is far more effective than trying to teach the infant words in which the infant is not interested at the moment.

While the infant is approximately six through ten months of age, there is continuous refinement in the establishment of joint reference between the adults who take care of the child and the infant. The later stages will overlap with the next crucial step: the onset of intentional communication.

Steps in the Development of Joint Reference

The major work on the development and function of joint reference has been carried out by Jerome Bruner. The following descriptions are adapted from his work (Bruner 1983).

In the earliest phases of joint attention, the adult simply looks at something nearby, and the infant, after looking at the adult's face, looks at the same thing. It may be an object (for example, a toy, stuffed animal, or the infant's crib) or an activity (for example, other children playing with a ball). By paying attention to the same thing at the same time, the infant and adult can share the experience of the object or event. That, in turn, allows the adult to provide examples of the words that go with the object or event. In this way, adults expose children to the connection between words and things.

An important change begins when the infant is about six months old. The child's interest in toys and objects increases, shifting away from looking at people's faces to looking at and manipulating objects. This change happens partly because the child's eye–hand coordination has improved, and infants can now reach, grasp, and manipulate the objects that interest them. However, the objects themselves, and sharing them with trusted adults, seem to be of special concern. At this age infants spend a lot of time and

effort trying to reach and take objects, to exchange them, and so on. As children become excited about all the new things to be found in the world, the children's interactions with adults become three-way; that is, the interactions include the infant, the adult, and some object of interest to the infant.

Although infants have learned that they can share attention toward an object or event with another person, they still do not share the activities with any intention to communicate about them. Before six to nine months of age, children may communicate by crying or reaching. Although caring adults interpret children's desires and intervene, children do not realize as they cry that their signals will serve a communicative purpose. The infants' early cries are automatic reactions to some internal feelings.

As children (between eight and twelve months of age) move from automatic to intentional communication, the sharing of joint reference changes. When they are about nine months old, children come to understand what it means when others point. If the adult points, the infant will look at the target and not just at the pointing hand (as would have happened earlier). Also at this stage, after looking at the target, the infant will look back at the adult, using feedback from the adult's face for confirmation that the infant was correct. The adult also often names the object to which he or she points.

During this entire period, the adult watches the infant's face more than the infant watches the adult. This monitoring provides a good model for all adults who provide care for infants, whether they are family members or infant care teachers. Monitoring is a hallmark of caregiver behavior with infants who are eight to sixteen months old. By monitoring the child's glances and signs of interest, the

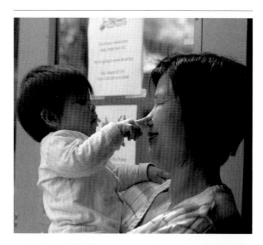

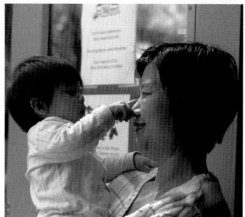

adult can interpret the environment for the child—providing the appropriate labels and setting the stage for labeling by the child.

Dr. Bruner points out that the crucial next phase is the emergence of the in-

fant's pointing. With this behavior infants begin to direct the attention of people around them and to check to see whether the people have understood. Infants will point, then look back and forth between the adult's face and the object to see whether the adult is looking at the object (that is, to see whether joint reference has been established). When the adult looks at the object to which a child points, they usually provide a label for the object. At this time the adult may also say, "Where's the _____?" Then the child will point to the object. This is usually followed by the adult's approval, often in the form of simple confirmation (for example, "That's right; there's the _____!"). Thus, the emergence of pointing coincides with the first signs of word comprehension.

Giving, showing, and especially pointing are the first conventional forms of communication. Prior to this time, infants and family members or teachers may have used a number of signals that they both understood, but anyone around children can understand what the children mean when they point. However, pointing is not yet symbolic (like words and some other gestures, which are described later in this section).

Early Vocal Play

As Dr. Sachs noted, six-month-old infants produce sounds in a pattern called babbling. Between six and seven months of age, babbling begins to change. A brief stage called vocal play occurs when children begin to experiment with long strings of syllable repetition. At this stage infants produce several sounds in one breath, and the infants begin to listen to others talking. Infant care teachers may hear things like "babababababa" and "dadadadada" or even "babadadabada." If the teacher responds to the child's sounds with a simple comment ("Yes, that's a nice doggie" or "Mmm, it feels good to have a dry diaper") or an imitation of the child's sounds, the infant is likely to repeat the sounds. However, the infant still does not connect the sound with meaning. Producing strings of sounds appears to be done simply because it is interesting and fun to do so, and it is even more interesting if the trusted adult joins in and then a turn-taking game spontaneously develops.

Onset of Intentional Communication—Eight to Twelve Months

Between eight and twelve months of age, infants change from using generalized signals (crying, whining, cooing, laughing) in an automatic, reflexive way to understanding that their signals have a clear and definite effect on others, and the infants begin to use conventional symbols to communicate their desires. The symbols include gestures (for example, opening and closing the hand to gesture "give me" or "I want"), vocalizations (for example, "ahahah" to accompany the "give me" gesture), and, finally, words.

Most infants about eight or nine months old begin to interact with caring adults with the goal of communicating something. This is one of the most important transitions in infancy: the onset of intentional communication. From now until the end of this developmental period, there will be continuous refinement in the child's attempts to communicate. An expert on communication in infancy, Elizabeth Bates, notes that the critical change is that children at this stage understand that their signals will have an effect on their listener and know what the effect will be (Bates and others 1979, 1988). Thus, infants become deliberate givers of signals about the things they need or want; they become more equal partners in the vital game of communication.

However, the conversational turns that children take at this stage will not neces-

sarily include words. Early communications are expressed primarily through gestures, which are present in three substages of the development of communication (Bates and others 1979). In the earliest substage, infants use conventional rituals to interact with teachers and other adults. The infants seem to take great delight in showing off for attention. They will play peek-a-boo, wave good-bye, give kisses, and shake the head for no.

Infants also use a lot of jargon (that is, long strings of unintelligible sounds with adult intonation patterns). The tone of voice makes the jargon sound like questions, commands, or statements, even though the infants do not utter understandable words. Before long, the infants interact with the adult by showing an object, but they are not willing to release it, even though the original intention appeared to be to give or share.

Finally, the infants go beyond simply showing to giving and pointing. In doing so they appear to be commenting on the object of interest or requesting that it be given to them. These gestures, postures, actions, and vocalizations (for example, "ahahah") are forms with which infants communicate what they will soon be able to say with words. For example, reaching with an opening and closing hand and saying "ahahah" to ask for a cookie will soon be replaced by pointing and an utterance, such as "wandat" or "cookie." This is clearly an important step for the infant, a quantum leap in the ability to have an effect on the environment.

The attempts by the infant at intentional communication should be recognized and reinforced. Dr. Bates and others (1979) note three clear signs of the presence of intentionality in infants:

1. The child begins to look back and forth between the goal and the adult while emitting the signal (which may be a sound or a gesture). This action occurs in the earliest attempts at intentional communication, when the child is unsure of the new skill. Once the child is confident that the adult is attending to the signal, the child's looking back and forth decreases in frequency and is repeated only when the adult fails to respond.

2. The child changes the signal, depending on the adult's response. The child expands, adds, and substitutes signals until the goal has been reached or clearly will not be reached. For example, on seeing an interesting object, the child may extend an arm toward it while opening and shutting the hand. If the adult does not give the object to her, the child may look back and forth between the object and the adult, say "eheheh," and continue to open and shut the extended hand. If that signal fails, the child may say "eheheh" louder and lean toward the object.

3. The form of the signals gradually changes toward abbreviated or exaggerated patterns that are appropriate only for communicating. For example, what begins as a reach and grasp is shortened to a quick open-and-shut movement of the hand, with the arm only partially extended. Because the child has had many experiences by this time with reaching and grasping in order to get objects, the purpose of the new abbreviated form may be only to enlist the adult's help. Similarly, grunts and fussing become ritualized into shorter, more regular sounds that shift in volume, depending on the adult's reaction (like the previous "eheheh" example). This latter development also suggests that the child recognizes the conventional aspect of communication. (Conventional, here, refers to the sounds or gestures whose functions are agreed on and recognized by both adult and child.) The sounds and gestures that become conventional are by-products of the child's emerging use of signals to communicate.

The new experience of being able to communicate intentions successfully is a powerful motive for the child to acquire language skills (Moerk 1977, 49). It is important that teachers recognize these attempts to communicate and use them as opportunities to further language and communication development by providing the appropriate labels, either in confirmation of the "comment" made by the child or in compliance with the child's "request."

Earlier in this section, a give-and-take, turn-taking aspect to adult–infant interaction from the very early stages was discussed. Many developmental psychologists (including Daniel Stern, Jerome Bruner, Elizabeth Bates, Susan Goldin-Meadow, and Michael Tomasello) believe that this give-and-take lays the critical foundation for participating in conversation. By viewing all attempts at communication this way, a teacher can stimulate language development even when the child has no words. The key is to treat all gestures and vocalizations as conversational turns. For example:

> *CHILD:* (Gives toy dog to teacher)
>
> *TEACHER:* "Thank you! What a nice doggie." (Pets the dog)
>
> *CHILD:* (Reaches for the dog) "Aha-hah."
>
> *TEACHER:* (Hands dog to child) "Here you are! Want to pet her?"

There is no harm in responding to the words the child has made up, although they are not words used in adult language. For example, if a child calls the blanket "lala," a teacher gives it to the child when she says "lala" and responds, "Here's your blanket."

Invented words are typical of children at this age and are an important sign that the children are developing as communicators. The children will later replace such words with words from the adult language. When children are this age, you want to show them that you understand and want to communicate with them in a positive way; you do not require that children use the adult word.

Use of Conventional Symbols— Twelve to Sixteen Months

During this period, children perfect their ability to get trusted adults to pay attention to them and the topics that interest them. Intentional communication is well

established. The children have made the important shift to the use of conventional symbols for communication. In the early stages, these symbols will be gestures as well as words.

About twelve months of age, children utter their first true words. These are likely to be words such as "mama," "dada," "papa," "da" (for dog), and "ba" (for bottle or baby). But the words may well be more idiosyncratic; for example, "ah" (hot) for cup or "moo" (moon) for outside. Usually, however, the words are used in the presence of the objects they represent, such as favorite toys, family members, or pets.

At the same time that first words appear, children begin to use a special class of gestures. The gestures (like first words) are made in the presence of particular objects but do not seem to be attempts to use the object for its real purpose. Examples include the child taking a toy cup and pretending to drink from it, holding a toy phone to the ear, taking a toy pillow from a doll crib and putting his head on it, or pretending to sleep. These gestures show that children

understand the purpose or functional use of the objects and have come to classify them in a conventional way. Thus, the gestures may be considered a primitive form of naming an object or action and a categorization of the object or action as belonging to a particular conceptual class. For this reason the gestures are called *recognitory gestures* (Bates and others 1979, 1988). The conceptual skills needed to use recognitory gestures are the same skills needed to use words. The skills are simply being demonstrated in a gestural modality instead of the vocal modality.

There is one major difference between the gestures and words, however. Children generally use recognitory gestures to identify things for themselves, rarely to communicate with others. But the gestures are still important. In the same way that you follow the children's direction of gaze and name the object of their gaze, you should apply a name to the object or

activity represented by children's gestures. For example:

There is one other class of gestures that you may see. These gestures are made far less frequently than recognitory gestures but are probably closer to a real word. These are empty-handed gestures carried out in the absence of an object (for example, making a turning movement with the hand to indicate turning a doorknob as a request to go outside). These gestures, too, should be responded to as though they were words. Indeed, all the gestures described in this section should be treated as though they were part of a conversational turn. Never discourage children from using them.

By twelve months of age, most children recognize their own name when it is spoken. They can also follow simple instructions, especially when accompanied by a visual cue (for example, "say bye-bye" accompanied by a wave). Children understand the word *no* and the *no* intonation and usually respond appropriately. Many children speak one or more words, although it is not uncommon for first words to occur as late as fifteen or sixteen months of age. Words, jargon, and babble all occur together. During the next year of life, children's words increase, and jargon and babbling disappear. (This further development of language is discussed in the next section.)

Although children twelve to sixteen months old may produce only a few words, the children usually understand more than they can say. It is not unusual for them to understand between 70 and

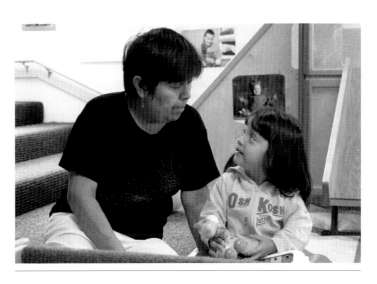

190 words. (These estimates are based on norms in *MacArthur-Bates Communicative Development Inventories: Words and Gestures* 2006.) *When* children begin to use words and *how* children produce words when they do start vary considerably. Some children retain sentence-like jargon mixed with words for quite some time; other children at this age begin to use single words, pronounced quite clearly. This variability reflects normal individual differences and is nothing to be concerned about.

Suggestions for Supporting Language Development

First, talking with the baby is important. For instance, say "hi" when approaching the infant and "bye" when leaving. Talk while bathing, diapering, and feeding the child. All these situations provide opportunities to establish and maintain joint reference; allow the child to communicate with gestures, vocalizations, and words; and provide the names for the objects and activities in the child's daily life.

Teachers can use "caregiver talk" (also called child-directed speech) with infants. As Jacqueline Sachs pointed out in the previous section, this way of talking helps maximize children's skills when children are very young. Caregiver talk consists of simple but grammatically correct sentences. The pitch of the voice is higher than when you talk to adults, and intonation patterns (the up-and-down pitch changes of the voice) are more exaggerated. In caregiver talk, you will also use more repetition of words than you use in speech to adults.

Second, use the child's ability to participate in joint reference to teach her about the things in the world around the child. Observe the child carefully so you can use a child's focus of attention as much as possible; that is, try to provide labels for or comment on things that the child is looking at, pointing to, and showing you. Avoid trying to direct her attention to another object or activity. When you notice that a child has followed your line of sight, it is also appropriate to label what you are looking at.

Use communicative modes, contexts, and intentions that are within the child's current competencies. Communicative modes used by children in this stage include gestures, sounds, body postures (for example, leaning forward in excitement), and words, usually produced within the context of game-like rituals or daily activities. A child's intention is usually to get the adult to pay attention to some object of interest or to do something for the child. Another way to set up contexts for joint reference that can be fun for both adult and child is to carry the child around on "word walks," pointing to and labeling objects and activities that are of interest to the child.

Third, provide opportunities for turn-taking, a critical part of language use. There are many ways to do this with children in a natural way during this stage. Everyday activities that demonstrate turn-taking can and should be done nonlinguistically (for example, physical play), vocally (for example, sound games, imitation), and linguistically (for example, words). The activity must be done without dominating the exchange of conversation. It is critical to remember that the goal is talking *with* children (that is, taking turns with them) rather than talking *to* them. Turn-taking routines in which the teacher keeps asking "What's that?" should be avoided because those routines provide dead-end avenues for the child. The only turn possible after such a question is the answer, and then the conversation is over.

Because infants and toddlers are new to participating in conversation, it is important that you provide sufficient opportunity for the children to take their turn. After you take a turn, wait for a response from the child with clear, visible anticipation. Respond once, then wait for the child to respond. Attend carefully to the child's behavior as a potential turn in the conversation; the child may be participating nonverbally. Treat all of the child's behavior as communicative, as a turn in a beginning conversation. To make sure that there is time for the child's turns, pay close attention to the child. Do not just rattle on. Keep your statements simple. Wait for the child's response; do not be afraid of a few seconds of silence. Here is an example of attentive turn-taking:

> *TEACHER:* "I see you looking at the doggie."
>
> (Pause)
>
> *TEACHER:* "He's big, huh!" (Or if the child said "doggie," the teacher could say, "Yes, a doggie!")
>
> (Pause) "What a big doggie."

Give-and-take games, such as peek-a-boo and pat-a-cake, which can be carried out with many variations, are excellent teaching tools. The games require roles, turn-taking, joint attention, and sequential structure while you and the child have a great time.

Fourth, read simple, short stories when the child is about twelve months old, and read only when the child is quiet and alert. Picture books with realistic photographs or clear, simple drawings of familiar objects are a good means of introducing the child to the abstract representation of real objects with which the child has had experience. Be careful to read only if the child is interested. Do not force a child to be quiet or sit still, and be careful to respond to the child as a real partner in the conversation about the book.

Fifth, when a child demonstrates ability at a given level, it may be appropriate to do what Jerome Bruner (1983) calls "upping the ante." In other words, you can encourage performance at that new level. For example, if the child knows the word *car* and asks for a toy car by reaching or making a sound, you can respond by

saying, "What do you want?" and pause briefly to allow the child to respond. The child may then say "car." However, if the child does not say the word, do not push the child to verbalize. Instead, the best approach is to name the item. For example, you may say, "Oh, you want the car." Pressuring the child to do or say something may discourage him from using language. In contrast, even when the child does not verbalize the "correct" word, your modeling of language encourages the child to participate in the next communicative interchange with you.

Reasons for Concern

All babies begin to babble when they are about six months old, including babies who are born deaf. However, babbling will not continue beyond eight or nine months of age if the baby cannot hear the language around her. If babbling stops, there is reason for concern. Dr. Sachs discusses this issue in detail in Section One and recommends important follow-up care if deafness or a less severe hearing impairment is suspected.

Children are inquisitive beings who want to share new discoveries with their trusted adults. A problem may be indicated (1) if a child does not show an interest in making new discoveries by interacting with objects and trusted adults in familiar environments; or (2) if the child does not engage in the typical, ritualized games of infancy, such as peek-a-boo and pat-a-cake.

By participating in joint-reference activities, children gain critical early experiences for language acquisition. Thus, other warning signs include (1) if a child, at nine or ten months of age, does not follow the direction of an adult's line of vision or pointing; or (2) if a child, by eleven or twelve months of age, does not give, show, and point to objects or does not engage in or initiate ritualized games with trusted adults. (See appendix B, "Reasons for Concern That Your Child or a Child in Your Care May Need Special Help," a brochure published by the California Department of Education.)

A child typically begins to use words when he or she is ten to fourteen months old. If a child does not use any words by the end of this period, the child should be watched carefully over the next few months to determine whether follow-up care is necessary.

References

Bates, Elizabeth, and others. 1979. *The Emergence of Symbols: Cognition and Communication in Infancy.* New York: Academic Press, Inc.

Bates, Elizabeth, and others. 1988. *From First Words to Grammar: Individual Differences and Dissociable Mechanisms.* New York: Cambridge University Press.

Bruner, Jerome. 1983. *Child's Talk: Learning to Use Language.* New York: W. W. Norton & Co., Inc.

Fenson, L., V. Marchman, P. Dale, D. Thal, and J. S. Reznick. 2006. *The MacArthur-Bates Communicative Development Inventories.* 2nd ed. Baltimore, MD: Brookes.

Goldin-Meadow, Susan. 2005. *The Resilience of Language.* New York: Taylor and Francis.

Moerk, Ernst. 1977. *Pragmatic and Semantic Aspects of Early Language Development.* Baltimore, MD: University Park Press.

Stern, Daniel. 1985. *The Interpersonal World of the Infant: A View from Psychoanalysis and Developmental Psychology.* New York: Basic Books, Inc.

———. 2002. *The First Relationship: Infant and Mother.* Rev. ed. Developing Child Series. Edited by Jerome Bruner and others. Cambridge, MA.: Harvard University Press.

Tomasello, Michael. 2003. *Constructing a Language.* Cambridge, MA: Harvard University Press.

Section Three:
The Older Infant

Introduction

This section describes the language and communication of the older infant. Wendy Wagner Robeson and Kathleen McCartney provide a comprehensive discussion of the unfolding of language during this expansive toddler period. The period from sixteen to thirty-six months of age marks immense growth and transition in young children's language and communication skills. At sixteen months of age, most children speak only one word at a time, although they may understand longer utterances addressed to them. By thirty-six months of age, most children are speaking complex sentences. To many parents, infant/toddler care teachers, researchers, and even to psycholinguists, this period of growth and transition seems nothing short of a miracle. Throughout this section, the authors suggest how the infant/toddler care teacher can nurture this important period of communication for the young child.

Wendy Wagner Robeson, Ed.D., is a senior research scientist at the Wellesley Centers for Women at Wellesley College. Her research focuses on links between language and social development, early care and education, and school readiness. She has been the principal investigator or co-principal investigator on many studies, including the NICHD Study of Early Child Care and Youth Development. She holds a doctorate in language development from Harvard Graduate School of Education.

Kathleen McCartney is Dean of the Harvard Graduate School of Education and the Gerald S. Lesser Professor in Early Childhood Development. She is a developmental psychologist whose research informs theoretical questions on early experience and development as well as policy questions on child care, early childhood education, poverty, and parenting. Since 1989, she has served as a principal investigator on the National Institute of Child Heath and Human Development (NICHD) Study of Early Child Care and Youth Development, a study of 1,350 children from birth through age sixteen. Findings from this study were summarized in *Child Care and Child Development* (2005). Dr. McCartney received her B.S. in psychology from Tufts University and her M.S. and Ph.D. in psychology from Yale University.

Emergence of Communication: Words, Grammar, and First Conversations

Wendy Wagner Robeson and Kathleen McCartney

Overview of Language and Communication Issues

The ability to communicate involves many overlapping skills. Initially, an infant will communicate through gestures, eye contact, and vocalizations. However, language offers the child greater flexibility in the messages that can be conveyed. In order to communicate, the young child must master the rules of both language and social interaction. The young child makes great progress toward mastering those rules from sixteen to thirty-six months of age. This mastery will continue through the child's school years.

Children need to learn the four major rule-governed systems of language and communication, which are (1) phonology, (2) semantics, (3) syntax, and (4) pragmatics.

1. *Phonology* refers to sound patterns. The young child needs to acquire the rules by which sounds are combined in the language. Over time, the child's pronunciation of words will become more and more adultlike. For example, in English, a child might say "lellow" for yellow. With time, the child will say the word just as adults do.

2. *Semantics* refers to the meaning of words. The young child needs to use agreed-on definitions. For example, a child might initially use the word *dog* to refer to all four-legged creatures. Through conversations and direct experiences, the child will eventually come to use words as other people do.

3. *Syntax* refers to the grammatical rules by which words are combined. The system of grammatical rules for all languages is complex. When children begin to create two-word utterances, they use a primitive rule system. Over time, this system comes to match the adult rule system. Some rules are mastered easily. For example, in English, children quickly learn that the rule to make a past-tense verb is usually to add *ed*

to the verb. Later they will learn the exceptions to this rule.

4. *Pragmatics* refers to the social rules of language. The child needs to learn how to use language to accomplish goals. In other words, the child needs to learn the various functions of language. For example, requests that are demands need to be made differently from requests that are polite inquiries.

How children acquire these rules is not clear. Certainly, language is learned through social experience. Yet children acquire certain skills with such great regularity that some researchers believe language is primarily a function of maturation (that is, language development occurs primarily from physiological growth rather than experience). Other researchers consider a multiple-factors approach to language development.

Stages of Language Communication

Children understand many words before they can say them. The term "productive language" refers to the language that children are able to say or produce on their own. The term "receptive language" refers to the language that children are able to understand or comprehend. The age when a child will begin to say words varies greatly—some children begin at ten months while others begin at eighteen months of age. These first words are both meaningful and intentional.

One-Word Stage

By sixteen months of age, most children are using language, one word at a time. The one-word stage is characterized by the following behaviors:

1. Babbling decreases, although it may continue until a child is about eighteen months of age.

2. For some children, their first words are related to things they can act on. The words may refer to objects or events that are familiar and important to them (for example, family members). Other words such as "no" or "mine" result from their interactions with others.

3. For some children, their first words may be shortened versions of phrases they have heard, such as "duhwanna" for "I don't want to." These expressions often function as socially appropriate ways to communicate with others.

Children's vocabulary quickly develops. By sixteen months, children may understand 50 to 150 words, but, on average, they may speak only seven to 15 different words. Later on, children will have what is known as vocabulary spurts and will learn many more words and use many more words in their conversations. These spurts usually occur around the age of eighteen to twenty-four months.

By the end of the one-word stage, a word may stand for a whole message. When one word is both meaningful and expresses complex pragmatic intentions, it is called a "holophrase." For example, a child might say "milk" to communicate the message of "I want more milk."

Two-Word Stage

Children's transition to the two-word stage occurs gradually between the ages of eighteen and thirty months (or about seven months after the first words were spoken). Again, there is great variability among children on when this takes place. Toddlers begin to string words together but do not include all the necessary grammar in their sentences. This stage is called telegraphic speech. A child's speech resembles a telegram; only the essential parts are included. Words that are left out include articles (for example, "the"), conjunctions (for example, "and"), prepositions (for example, "over"), and helping verbs (for example, "to be"). For instance, a child might say "put shoe foot" for "put the shoe on my foot" or "baby sleep" for "the baby is sleeping." Even so, the child's language is rule-governed, although the rules are not as sophisticated as the adult rule system children will eventually acquire. The early two-word utterances are short and simple. At this stage, as with all stages of communication, teachers and others must make every effort to understand the intentions of a child's speech.

Multiword Stage (Sentences)

With time, children's sentences grow longer, become more varied and more complex, and contain more and more words. Between the ages of two and four years, children begin to form grammatically correct sentences, although their rule system is still not complete. As the sentences become longer, they become syntactically more complex. Children typically use consistent patterns that sound different from the way adults talk. For example, as they learn to ask questions, many children use sentences such as "Where kitty is hiding?" or "Why the lady can't go?" Do not think of these sentence constructions as mistakes. They are really signs that children are working out the complex rules of the language.

By three years of age, the child's vocabulary consists of more than 300 words. This vocabulary explosion is accompanied by the growth in three-word or longer utterances. The child at this stage has moderately complex speech and is more mature in thought and social interactions. Multiword utterances use more sophisticated language. Their sentences involve more complex syntax and more semantic knowledge. The child can talk about the past, present, and future and has learned how to use language to get things done. However, there still are differences between the child's language and

young children, are common in almost every language. This conversational style used with children has been referred to as "baby talk," "motherese," or, more precisely, "child-directed speech."

Child-Directed Speech

Child-directed speech can be identified by eight key features (Snow 1986). An adult using child-directed speech:

1. speaks with clear pronunciation;
2. speaks at a slower rate;
3. speaks in shorter sentences;
4. repeats the same utterance two or more times;
5. speaks in a higher-than-normal pitch;
6. uses simple words;
7. speaks with exaggerated intonation so that the speech has a singsong quality;
8. speaks in grammatically simple sentences.

There is some debate about the functions of child-directed speech. Some researchers believe its function is to signal to the child that communicating will be easier to "practice" now. Other researchers believe that adults continuously fine-tune the complexity of their language to a child's level of understanding—this is why an adult will speak differently to a baby or a toddler. This debate about why adults use child-directed speech when talking to young children mostly concerns the child's development of syntax. There seems to be little debate over whether children profit from meaningful language exchanges with the adults in their lives. In one child care study, children whose teachers engaged them in verbal interaction scored higher on four measures of language and communication. Verbal interaction among peers was not positively associated with language development.

the adult's. For example, children may overuse a word (calling all four-legged animals dogs") or underuse a word (using "dog" to refer only to a particular dog).

Caregiver Talk

When adults speak to young children, they speak in a manner different from the way they speak to other adults. The way adults talk to babies differs from talk to toddlers, which differs from talk to preschoolers. Adults adapt their language so it is easier to understand. These speech adjustments by adults, which seem to occur automatically to help adults talk with

Although peers serve an important social function, the verbal environment peers provide cannot replace that of more experienced communicators, such as teachers and parents (McCartney 1984).

Infant/Toddler Care Teacher Strategies

Teachers can use a number of strategies to promote language development and communication. To test skill in promoting language, teachers may ask themselves the following questions (see also Mattick 1981; Robeson 1994). The answer to every question should be yes.

1. Am I involved in a back-and-forth interaction?

   Sometimes adults engage in monologues rather than in real communication. As a teacher, you should encourage the child to engage in conversations. It is important to think of the child as a conversational partner and to check who is doing the most talking—you or the child.

2. Am I really listening to what the child is saying?

   You should not interrupt the child as soon as you think you know what has been said. By listening carefully, you can ask the child for more details and give the child alternatives to consider. Your replies to the child will signal that you understood what the child was trying to say. Or your replies can signal that there was a breakdown between the conversational partners.

3. Do I finish my sentences and thereby my thoughts?

   If you want to be understood by the child and be a good language model, try not to leave the child hanging during conversations. Communication with the young child is a form

of social interaction. Through such interactions, the child's language will continue to grow.

4. Do I avoid using the same phrase in my interactions with the child, such as "That's nice" or "Good job"?

   The use of pat answers does nothing to promote verbal interaction between the child and you. Children will also learn that you use the same replies no matter what they say or ask—and that sometimes the teacher makes no sense. It is important to really listen to what the young child is saying or asking and use a variety

of expressions that cause children to think. Your relationship with a child should be nurturing, positive, stimulating, and responsive; pat answers have no place in such a relationship.

5. Do I provide opportunities that encourage verbal interactions?

Children should be engaged in activities that naturally lead to verbal interaction with both you and other children. Such activities include mealtime, free play indoors and outdoors, personal care routines, looking at books or listening to stories, picture discussions, and informal conversations. Take time to follow children's interests and focus on providing child-driven activities.

6. Do I initiate one-to-one conversations with individual children concerning everyday events?

It is important to have individual conversations with children. They can talk about events that are happening now in their lives. Older children can talk about the past and future as well. These conversations show children that you think children are worth listening to. Also, the one-to-one conversations give children who are shy a chance to talk with you.

7. Do I make an effort to understand what a child is trying to say?

You may have to make extra efforts to understand some children because their pronunciation is unclear or because they are still at the one- or two-word stage. You need to make the effort because children will begin to acquire communicative competence if they are able to get the message of their utterances or their intention across to you. Once children realize that you take the time to understand why they are trying to communicate, they will talk

more and their language will grow. Your speech to the child needs to be semantically contingent, which means you need to stay on the child's topic.

8. Do I allow a child to finish a sentence?

Although you may be tempted to finish children's sentences for them, it is important not to do so. Children need to figure out how to communicate their messages effectively. This will never happen if someone else always completes their sentences. Once children finish, make sure to respond.

9. Do I promote self-confidence in the child as a communicator?

When you actively listen to the child, let the child finish what is being said, and try to understand what the child is saying, you promote self-confidence in the child as a communicator. With self-confidence the child will be willing to risk other attempts at communication. Communication occurs through rich interaction between children and adults.

10. Do I model grammatically correct language?

As the teacher, you serve as a language model for children. Therefore, try to use grammatically correct language. But do not put grammar before everything else, as social interaction is central to the development of communicative skills and language. Grammatical correction should not interfere with a warm and social relationship between the adult and child.

11. Do I expand and extend the child's language?

You should listen to the child and try to expand the child's language and extend the topic that the child raised in the conversation. When you *expand* the child's language, you repeat what the child has said but make it grammatically correct. This implicit feedback turns the ungrammatical child utterance into something grammatically correct. For example, a child may say "That be monkey," and the teacher would say, "That is a monkey." When you *extend* a topic, you partially repeat what the child has said but also add more information. Extensions happen more often with older children, who are easier to understand. For example, a child may say "fire truck," and the teacher would say, "That's your new fire truck."

When to Encourage Language and Communication

A sensitive teacher who pays close attention to an individual child will know from the child's behavior when he is ready, interested, and motivated to engage in language activities and conversation. When the child is ready, nearly every exchange can be used to encourage language and communication. This even includes time spent on diapering, toileting, and self-care. Teachers should talk to the children and not just to other adults. As will be clear, some situations seem to lend themselves particularly well to language interaction. These activities can involve a teacher with one child or with more children (Maxim 1980).

Storytelling

Children enjoy stories, either told or read aloud. At first it is important that the stories are about things familiar to the children. Short books with simple concepts and clear pictures are best at this stage. As children develop, they will also enjoy stories about make-believe, humor, new places, and exotic animals. With short books, have children point to pictures and talk about what they see. Stories are valuable because they (1) expose children to rich and varied language; (2) help children discover new words, meanings, and understandings; and (3) promote imaginative thought. Story time also sets the foundation for children's literacy development.

Picture Discussions

A picture file can consist of large, colorful, uncomplicated pictures that stimulate verbal exchanges. The pictures can come from magazines, old calendars, advertisements, and discarded books. They should be clear and not have confusing details. The pictures should be attached to construction paper or card stock. A good way to protect pictures and lengthen their "life" is to laminate them

or cover them with clear, contact paper. These pictures can be posted in the room at the child's eye level, used to make a picture book, or used by the children to talk about what they see and what they think about the picture. Discussions about pictures are valuable because they (1) motivate children to discuss what they see, and (2) inspire children to make up stories. Teachers must form their questions in a way that moves children from stating what they see to discussing the picture at higher levels of interpretation. Instead of asking "what," also ask "why." Children can also make up stories from a series of pictures.

Make-believe and Fantasy Play

Toddlers love make-believe and fantasy play. An activity area or center that includes a variety of simple dress-up materials and other thematic props (for example, a toy camera or cooking utensils) sets the stage for children's fantasy play. Having puppets available also encourages children to use language through pretend play. Puppets can be used in teacher-initiated activities in one-on-one or small-group situations. Including blocks may encourage more cross-gender

play so that both boys and girls make use of the center. Make sure to change the props periodically as interest in them dwindles so that children can stretch their imagination.

Informal Conversations

Children should be encouraged to speak freely both to the teacher and to other children. The teacher provides verbal stimulation to help children associate language with their experiences. These conversations might occur anywhere: during mealtimes, in the dramatic play area, or in the sandbox. Children's vocabulary, language skills, and world knowledge grow through conversations with responsive and caring adults (Burns, Griffin, and Snow 1999).

Reasons for Concern

As we have stressed, there is great variation in the age at which children begin to talk and the rate at which language development proceeds. However, some children may stand out noticeably from their age group because of their language development. This is especially the case when a child's language delay seems to be causing problems with her cognitive or social development. Children with delayed language development have limited vocabularies, and their sentence structure is less varied compared with other children their age. They may make more grammatical errors and have difficulty combining different kinds of information in single sentences. They may have problems talking about the future. They may misunderstand questions and often are misunderstood. They may use short, simple sentences and have difficulty maintaining a conversation (Dumtschin

1988). Their language delays can involve their receptive or productive language skills or both (Reich 1986). It is important to detect early language delays and provide intervention because language is so important for the child's continuing development.

Teachers are not speech–language pathologists and cannot diagnose problems or decide on the appropriate therapy. However, if at any age, especially three years of age, a child does not seem to be developing language typically, the teacher may suggest to the child's parents that they consult their child's doctor or appropriate professional. The American Speech-Language-Hearing Association (ASHA) can provide information related to language problems in young children (e.g., information about qualified audiologists and speech language pathologists). The ASHA is located in Rockville, MD, and can be reached by calling 1-800-638-8255 or by visiting its Web site (http://www.asha.org).

References

Burns, M. S., P. Griffin, and C. E. Snow, eds. 1999. *Starting Out Right: A Guide to Promoting Children's Reading Success.* Washington, DC: National Research Council.

Dumtschin, J. U. 1988. "Recognize Language Development and Delay in Early Childhood," *Young Children* 43 (1988): 16–24.

Mattick, I. 1981. "The Teacher's Role in Helping Young Children Develop Language Competence," in *Language in Early Childhood Education* (revised edition). Edited by Courtney B. Cazden. Washington, DC: National Association for the Education of Young Children, pp. 107–25.

Maxim, George W. 1980. *The Very Young: Guiding Children from Infancy Through the Early Years.* Belmont, CA: Wadsworth Publishing Co.

McCartney, K. 1984. "The Effect of Quality of Day Care Environment Upon Children's Language Development," *Developmental Psychology* 20 (1984): 244–60.

Reich, P. A. 1986. *Language Development.* Englewood Cliffs, NJ: Prentice Hall.

Robeson, W. W. 1994. "The Relationship Between Verbal Feedback from Mothers and Their Children's Language Development." PhD diss., Harvard University, Cambridge, MA.

Snow, C. E. 1986. "Conversations with Children," in *Language Acquisition: Studies in First Language Development.* 2nd ed. Edited by Paul Fletcher and Michael Garman. New York: Cambridge University Press, pp. 69–89.

Section Four:
The Bilingual Child Care Setting

Introduction

*I*n this section, Dr. Eugene E. García recommends actions infant care teachers can take to ensure a supportive, responsive environment in which communication thrives. He also explores and dispels some of the common but inaccurate myths about a child learning more than one language early in life. He makes a strong point about supporting the child's home or native language during the early development of the child's language and communication skills. In addition, Dr. García discusses the importance of communicating frequently with parents about their child, using the native language of the family in both formal and informal communication. The implications for multilingual child care settings are also described.

Dr. Eugene García is Vice President for Education Partnerships at Arizona State University (ASU). He held the position of Dean at ASU's College of Education from 2002 to 2006, and before coming to ASU, he was Dean and Professor of the Graduate School of Education at the University of California, Berkeley. He also served as Co-director of the National Center for Research on Cultural Diversity and Second Language Acquisition at the University of California, Santa Cruz, where previously he was Professor of Education. Dr. García has published extensively in the area of language teaching and bilingual development. He served as Senior Officer and Director of the Office of Bilingual Education and Minority Languages Affairs in the U.S. Department of Education from 1993 to 1995. He served as chair of the National Task Force on Early Childhood Education for Hispanics from 2005 to 2008. He is presently conducting research in the areas of effective schooling for linguistically and culturally diverse student populations.

Caring for Infants in a Bilingual Child Care Setting

Eugene E. García

Caring for young children is one of the most important activities in society because young children's early experiences establish their ability to learn throughout life. This is particularly true of infants' language development (Shonkoff and Phillips 2000). Language provides a vital and complex social repertoire that allows young children to understand and influence their environment. The types of interactions that toddlers and infants have with caring adults can affect their language development (Rudd et al.

2008) and therefore their ability to learn in subsequent years. Researchers have concluded that the infant/toddler care and education field has had a positive effect on the school readiness of young children. However, the effects have been "limited" in language development for all children, including infants whose families speak a language other than English at home. Therefore, they recommend designing and modifying infant/toddler strategies concerned with promoting greater language development for children learning English (National Task Force on Early Childhood Education for Hispanics 2007). This paper aims to do just that by making recommendations for professionals in infant/toddler educational settings working with infants whose families do not speak English at home.

The Importance of the Child's Home Language

First and foremost, infants and toddlers need a rich linguistic environment in order to thrive and develop their language and communication competence. The first three sections of this guide describe in detail the development of language for the child from birth to three years of age and the critical role of the infant care teacher in supporting and enhancing that development. When an infant or toddler is first learning language, adults should provide a rich linguistic environment, both at home and in the child care setting, that supports the native language and the culture of the infant's family (Petersen, Jones, and McGinley 2008). This statement is true regardless of the family's language or cultural group. When infants are cared for by the family, the native language and culture are supported automatically. However, when children are cared for outside the family, the native language of the infant care teacher(s) may or may not match that of the infant. In 2000, almost a fifth (18 percent) of individuals ages five and older reported speaking a language other than English at home (García and Cuellar 2006). The fact that English is the prevailing language in many child care settings in the United States raises some concerns and issues that need to be considered.

Preserving a family's home language and cultural heritage is very important to the identity and sense of well-being of the entire family. For young children, cultural and linguistic identity provides a strong sense of self and family belonging

(Gonzalez 2001). This sense of self and belonging, in turn, supports a wide range of learning capabilities, not the least of which is learning a second language (García 2005; Cummins 2000). Another important consideration is the relationship of language development and learning about one's culture. Language learning for the young child is closely tied to cultural learning. The specific issues of culture as they relate to language are discussed in Section Five.

Given the cultural and language diversity of infants and toddlers being cared for outside the family, how can infant/toddler care teachers best support and enrich each child's native language in a bilingual child care setting?

First, all child care programs need well-trained, sensitive teachers who speak the same language as the child and represent the child's cultural group. Although this is not a current reality, it is a goal to strive for to support all children and families in the United States. Presently, there are efforts to encourage states to establish early learning guidelines for infants and toddlers that address these issues (Petersen, Jones, and McGinley 2008).

Second, and equally important, all teachers need to become educated about and sensitive to the issues of language and culture regardless of their own language background and cultural heritage (Petersen, Jones, and McGinley 2008; García 2005; Espinosa 1995). This understanding and sensitivity will support children, families, and child care providers as children grow and develop in a culturally diverse society.

Third, infant care teachers need to understand several important characteristics of the early bilingual experience to provide the most effective care to children in nonnative language environments.

This section explores several important issues:

- Actions that infant care teachers can take to ensure a supportive, responsive environment in which communication thrives
- Myths about the supposed negative effects of bilingualism
- Communication with the family and an understanding of the family's social circumstances

Providing a Supportive Language-Learning Environment

The optimal situation for supporting native-language learning is one in which the infant care teacher's language matches that of the infant and the infant's family. Providing the native language in the caregiving situation supports and reinforces the many rich encounters with language that the infant has within the family. As children begin speaking, it is important that they be exposed to and use their native language in a wide variety of ways because language and intellectual development are closely related.

When young children hear their native language spoken in familial settings and in the wider community, they are exposed to more words, more complex grammar, and more complex ideas, thoughts, and concepts. This broad range of linguistic and cognitive experiences in natural situations enriches the development of both language and intellectual functioning in the older infant and preschool child (Heath 1986).

Infants develop and thrive linguistically in rich but natural communication interactions. Rogoff (2003) argues that children internalize language and other important cultural ways of interacting through "guided participation," which may not include explicit teaching. In other words, infant care teachers should

not formally teach any language. What infant care teachers do naturally is what supports children's learning of their native language.

We also know that infants are like sponges in the sense that they "receive" language and store an incredible amount of language long before they "produce" spoken language. Activities such as telling stories, singing, rhyming, reading, and chanting in the child's home language, along with generally talking with the baby, support language development (Petersen, Jones, and McGinley 2008). Important differences in the language and cognitive development of infants and toddlers were recently documented in a nationwide Early Head Start study. Children who were read to frequently and regularly from the time they were fourteen months old showed greater language and cognitive development at thirty-six months than did children who were not read to in this way (Raikes et al. 2006).

These activities "bathe" the infant in a rich linguistic environment. The nonverbal communication that accompanies spoken language is also powerful and communicates an emotional context for the language experiences.

It is important for the infant/toddler care teacher who speaks the child's home language to communicate in a variety of ways, especially with the older infant and toddler. In one-to-one interactions with the young and mobile infant, the infant care teacher will speak intimately with the child, using informal language forms and simple, familiar words. As the infant gets older, the infant care teacher's communication about objects and activities in the environment and use of words and language forms will naturally become more diverse and varied. The teacher will model yet another form and context for language when she speaks with the child's family members and other teachers.

In all of these different conversations, the child receives exposure to language and communication in his or her native language. This exposure to vocabulary and grammar in a natural setting provides the child with a firm foundation in the native language. And this foundation enables the child to learn a second language more easily (García 2005; Cummins 2000).

But what if it is impossible to provide native-language or bilingual teachers? Will not this harm the linguistic development of the infants? Certainly, if the infant care teacher refuses to interact with the infant by ignoring the child's natural communicative attempts, the infant will soon stop communicating. However, more than 60 percent of any communicative act is nonverbal. Infants communicate initially by pointing, crying, wiggling, nodding, grimacing, and so on. The best approach to handling a language mismatch is for the teacher to attend to all the infant's communicative signals and to respond naturally with understanding and a visible willingness to communicate.

Regardless of the language environment, all infants attempt communication. Young children have not yet learned to be afraid of making mistakes; infants will "risk" communicating with infant care teachers regardless of the language the infants speak. Teachers should do the same. The child will not be confused by the use of an unfamiliar language by the teacher as long as that communication is authentic.

Teachers can help with the language mismatch by playing recordings of stories, rhymes, and songs in the child's native language. Toys, photos, pictures, and books that show the child's home culture will give the child things to point out, name, and talk about in his native language.

Still, it is important to find someone who can speak the infant's native language even if that person cannot be the child's primary caregiver in the child care program. The infant must feel welcome in this nonhome environment. Hearing her language will assist greatly. However, infant care teachers whose native language is different from the child's should never fear that their language is "bad" for the child and should not hesitate to speak to the child just as they would to infants from their own language group. The language mismatch is simply not optimal for the child's overall language and cognitive development.

Dismissing Myths About Bilingualism

Current research shows that bilingualism is not harmful; young children are quite capable of learning more than one language (García 2005). However, as discussed earlier, a firm foundation in the home language is recommended before the young child learns a second language. The very young child should be given every opportunity to learn the home language fully. This means that optimally, from birth to age four, children are cared

for in settings that support their native or home language.

However, because many young children are exposed to a nonnative language when they are cared for outside their homes, it is important to dispel some commonly held myths about the effects of bilingualism. What does bilingualism add or subtract in the "arithmetic" of language development? Is bilingualism bad? Does it lead to linguistic delays, communicative confusion, or other developmental risks? The early research on the effects of bilingualism painted a bleak picture. For instance, in 1952 one researcher concluded, "There can be no doubt that the child reared in a bilingual environment is handicapped in his language growth" (see Hakuta 1986). In essence, this understanding of bilingualism concluded that learning one language is hard enough, so learning two must be at least twice as hard, particularly for the young child.

Present-day research has shown this conclusion to be false, a myth perpetuated by misunderstood "common sense." Up-to-date research has shown that young children who live in supportive and nurturing bilingual environments do not suffer linguistically from those environments. This research has carefully documented the development of several types of bilingualism and compared the results to the development of English in monolingual children. Analysis of these comparisons clearly indicates that bilingual children, at both early and late periods of development, do not differ significantly from monolingual children. Genesee (2008, 34) asserts that "bilingual acquisition is not a burden on infants' and toddlers' capacity to acquire language."

An interesting and important finding, sometimes negatively interpreted, is that bilingual children may move through a phase of language mixing. The children are sometimes observed to use two languages as if they were one. For example, a Spanish/English bilingual child may say "Yo quiero *play*" (I want to *play*) or "Yo estaba *playendo*" (I was *playing*). In such cases, the child is using English vocabulary or grammar within a Spanish linguistic context. In the past, such instances of mixed language usage were interpreted as evidence of language confusion or the lack of vocabulary in one language. Today we understand those mixed-language instances as normal developmental occurrences and reflecting dual-language

competence (Genesee 2008; Soltero and Reyes 2008; García 2005; Reyes 2004).

Although bilingualism was once considered a "bad habit," best eliminated as soon as possible, today we can rest easy about the supposed harm bilingualism causes and instead appreciate and support the communicative development of the bilingual child. But if bilingualism is not harmful, should it be promoted? Should non-English-speaking infants hear as much English as possible? Should they receive early and consistent exposure to English so they can begin to acquire the English they will need to be successful in this country? Should child care providers attempt to teach English to non-English-speaking infants? Is an English-speaking care situation early in life exactly what is needed?

If the family's native language is not English, each of these questions can be answered with a clear no. We now know that the better a young child learns the native language and the many cognitive and social skills needed to communicate effectively in that language, the better the child will master the complexities of communicating in a second language (García 2005; Lopez and Greenfield 2004).

Communicating with Families

By exchanging information, family members can help infant/toddler care teachers provide an environment that supports native-language learning in infants and toddlers (Gonzalez, Moll, and Amanti 2005). When the family's native language is not English, they often prefer to exchange information with the child's infant care teacher in their native language. A number of formal and informal activities and strategies can aid the communication between teacher and family when the two have different native languages. When information must be given to families in a formal setting (for example, in a workshop on child care or state regulations), it should be provided by a professional who speaks the family's native language. All families appreciate these kinds of informational and educational sessions. But some families will often understand the information only if it is presented in their native language.

Informal situations for interaction can be quite useful. Providing a "family corner," perhaps, with simple refreshments for family members when they drop off or pick up children, allows for conversation in which infant care teachers and family members can chat about the day's happenings or community events. This kind of informal setting is much more tolerant of linguistic diversity. The informal interactions allow each participant, teacher, and family member alike to learn and practice aspects of a language that is foreign to him or her. Parents always appreciate it when teachers learn and use greetings and other simple phrases in the family's native language.

The family must be kept informed at all times of the relevant activities, moods, and health of their infant. To accomplish this, the teacher and family must communicate in the family's native language. In some situations, an older bilingual child can serve as an interpreter, although this may place the bilingual child in an awkward situation in which she cannot serve as an effective interpreter. Children should not be relied on to inform the family. Bilingual adults should always be used in such cases.

It may also be necessary to communicate with people other than the infant's parents, because many families count on older siblings, aunts, uncles, or grandparents to serve as primary caregivers. Any formal written communication, such as letters, forms, or newsletters, should be in the family's native language (Espinosa 1995). Infant/toddler care teachers may be perceived as members of the extended family. This role requires a much different communicative style from the one that is usually expected in formal caregiving situations. Families are likely to invite infant care teachers to family gatherings and celebrations. Although missing gatherings and celebrations would not usually be viewed negatively, attending such events may enhance the positive communicative relationship that is so important in a caregiving situation.

The Challenge of Diversity

An unfortunate social circumstance often reported in child care settings with bilingual and non-English-speaking children is the teacher's tendency to perceive the children and their families as foreigners. The noticeable fact that the children and their families usually do not speak English marks them as "different," and this observed difference sometimes leads to the teacher's negative feelings and treatment, perhaps stemming from a sense of defensiveness and suspicion. Such uncomfortable social situations often lead to the teacher's desire to change the difference by ridding children and their families of those attributes that make them different. Unfortunately, such attempts arouse only suspicion and negative reactions from the infants and their families. Rather than attempting to minimize diversity, everyone can be enriched by appreciating and respecting diversity.

Appreciating the significance and validity of the child's and family's language and culture is a challenge in itself. But today, when such a large number of children from diverse language and cultural groups are experiencing early

child care, that appreciation must be transformed into actions. Teachers must go beyond acknowledging diversity and help create environments where children's "funds of knowledge" are acknowledged and incorporated into everyday practices (Gonzalez, Moll, and Amanti 2005). Having teachers from the cultural and linguistic backgrounds of the families in need of child care is the key. If the child care program staff is unable to communicate with the child and family in their home language, the staff should refer, whenever possible, the family to a program that can.

Meeting the challenge of language and cultural diversity creates conflict, some of it inevitable and some of it unnecessary. Attitudes of condescension can be viewed as a signal to children and their families to abandon their language and culture in favor of English and the mainstream culture. Teachers who emphasize the mainstream values (even unknowingly) pull children away from the important linguistic and social resources available in the family and community. As a result, some family members may become wary of placing their children in caregiving situations that do not emphasize and practice their own values, traditions, and language. Other families may come to believe that only if they abandon their language and culture will their children succeed in American society. A family should not lose their rich cultural heritage because of someone's insensitive attitude and incorrect understanding about language development.

The obvious solution to this predicament seems simple: ensure that infant/toddler care teachers come from representative linguistic and cultural groups and that they use their personal and professional expertise to achieve the supportive ambience necessary for infant growth and development. In many child care settings, however, this simple solution is not yet possible. In programs where the staff does not have the same language and cultural background as the children served, the teachers' increased understanding and appreciation of the linguistic and cultural diversity of the children will create a positive caregiving context for the infant, the family, and the staff.

Such an environment requires staff members to set aside their misconceptions about the linguistic and cultural groups with whom they have had limited contact. In addition, staff members must be willing to learn from the children and the families they serve. Infant care teachers who serve linguistically diverse populations and who learn the family's language will be deeply appreciated; their efforts will be seen as a signal of acceptance and respect.

In today's increasingly diverse society, where minorities are fast becoming majorities, unfounded stereotypes and condescension have no place in an infant care program. The teachers' commitment to and respect for diversity can be translated into a highly supportive child care atmosphere in which children and families thrive.

Conclusion

By understanding and appreciating the issues discussed, the teacher can make the provision of care to infants from bilingual and non-English-speaking homes a rewarding experience. The following practices are recommended for teachers:

1. Provide a secure communicative environment for all children. The goal, whenever possible, is for the child's primary caregiver to speak the native language of the family and to reflect the family's cultural heritage. When this is not possible, it is important to find some regular assistance from others who speak the family's or infant's native language. When speaking to the infant in a language other than the infant's, use your native language as a natural communicative tool.
2. "Bathe" infants in a rich linguistic environment. Provide many opportunities for verbal and nonverbal communication, both listening to and watching the child and responding with the voice, facial expres-

sions, and gestures. Music, stories, and other communicative means expose the child to and engage the child in a wide variety of language and communication.
3. Set aside all negative myths and misunderstandings about bilingualism.
4. Communicate effectively with the infant's family—formally, informally, and frequently—in their native language.
5. Have a great time!

References

Cummins, James. 2000. *Language, Power, and Pedagogy: Bilingual Children in the Crossfire*. Clevedon, UK: Multilingual Matters.

Espinosa, Linda. 1995. "Hispanic Parent Involvement in Early Childhood Programs." ERIC Digest, Urbana, IL: ERIC Clearinghouse on Elementary and Early Childhood Education. (No. ED382412).

García, Eugene E. 2005. *Teaching and Learning in Two Languages:*

Bilingualism and Schooling in the United States. New York: Teachers College Press.

García, Eugene E., and Delis Cuellar. 2006. "Who Are These Linguistically and Culturally Diverse Students?" *Teachers College Record* 108(11): 2220–46.

Genesee, Fred. 2008. *Dual Language Development in Preschool Children.* Princeton, NJ: National Institute for Early Education Research Symposium on Early Education of ELL Students. March 12, 2008.

González, Norma. 2001. *I Am My Language: Discourses of Women and Children in the Borderlands.* Tucson: The University of Arizona Press.

González, Norma, Luis Moll, and Cathy Amanti. 2005. *Funds of Knowledge: Theorizing Practices in Households, Communities, and Classrooms.* Mahwah, NJ: Lawrence Erlbaum Associates.

Hakuta, Kenji. 1986. *Mirror of Language: The Debate on Bilingualism.* New York: Basic Books.

Heath, Shirley Brice. 1986. "Sociocultural Contexts of Language Development," in *Beyond Language: Social and Cultural Factors in Schooling Language Minority Students* (pp. 143–186). Sacramento: California State Department of Education.

Lopez, Lisa, and Daryl Greenfield. 2004. "The Cross-Language Transfer of Phonological Skills of Hispanic Head Start Children," *Bilingual Research Journal* 28 (1): 1–18.

National Task Force on Early Childhood Education for Hispanics. 2007. *Expanding and Improving Early Educa-*

tion for Hispanics: Executive Report. Tempe: Arizona State University.

Petersen, Sandra, Lynn Jones, and Karen A. McGinley. 2008. *Early Learning Guidelines for Infants and Toddlers: Recommendations to States.* Washington, DC: Zero to Three.

Raikes, H., B. A. Pan, G. Luze, C. S. Tamis-LeMonda, J. Brooks-Bunn, J. Constantine, L. B. Tarullo, H. A. Raikes, and E. T. Rodriguez. 2006. "Mother-Child Book Reading in Low-Income Families: Correlates and Outcomes During the First Three Years of Life," *Child Development* 77 (4): 924–53.

Reyes, Illiana. 2004. "Functions of Code Switching in Schoolchildren's Conversations," *Bilingual Research Journal* 28 (1): 77–98.

Rogoff, Barbara. 2003. *The Cultural Nature of Human Development.* New York: Oxford University Press.

Rudd, Loretta C., David W. Cain, and Terrill F. Saxon. 2008. "Does Improving Joint Attention in Low-Quality Child-Care Enhance Language Development?" *Early Child Development and Care* 178 (3): 315–38.

Shonkoff, Jack, and Deborah Phillips, eds. *From Neurons to Neighborhoods: The Science of Early Childhood Development.* Washington, DC: National Academies Press.

Soltero, Lucinda, and Iliana Reyes. 2008. Preschool English Language Learners' Early Literacy Development: Challenges and Possibilities from a Sociocultural Perspective. American Educational Research Association Annual Meeting, New York, March 27, 2008.

Section Five:
Culture and Communication

Introduction

In this section, Janet Gonzalez-Mena describes the basic elements of culture that influence language development and communication for infants and toddlers, such as when and how children begin to learn culturally appropriate nonverbal communication. She also discusses contrasting conversational styles and cultural differences in emphasis between verbal and nonverbal communication. The section closes with a consideration of differences in perceptions of how and what babies should learn.

Janet Gonzalez-Mena is a writer, consultant in early childhood education, and former community college instructor with experience as an early childhood education practitioner. Gonzalez-Mena is author of the PITC publication *A Guide to Routines* and several college textbooks on early childhood education. She co-authored two articles with Initisar Shareef: one for *Exchange* magazine that focused on their experience of conducting PITC training, and one for the NAEYC journal *Young Children* about cultural perspectives on discipline. Gonzalez-Mena obtained an MA degree in human development from Pacific Oaks College and did an internship under Magda Gerber at the Children's Health Council in Palo Alto, California. More recently she has been studying the Pikler approach to infant/toddler care and has visited the Pikler Institute in Budapest, Hungary, several times. Infants have been an important part of Janet's life; she raised five children of her own and has studied infant/toddler caregiving for the past 30 years.

Culture and Communication in the Child Care Setting

Janet Gonzalez-Mena

There is much more to communication than just spoken words. Even when people share the same language, cultural differences can have a great influence on whether the person receiving the message understands it in the way the sender intended.

For example, a toddler care teacher is down at eye level with two toddlers

What do you do when your professional knowledge about what children need differs from the culture of a family (or families) in your child care program? The answer to that question is simple, though it may not be easy: Communicate about the differences. Do not throw out what you know; expand on it. Help families increase their knowledge base while respecting who they are and what they believe. The important issue is to keep infants and toddlers connected to their culture while learning how to operate outside it.

who are splashing water while washing their hands. "Keep the water in the sink, please," says the teacher. The first toddler looks up at the teacher. The second child looks away. Though neither child stops splashing because of what the teacher said, the teacher assumes that the first

child was paying attention to her words, but the other was not. The teacher may be right, but she may also be wrong. Another teacher may get a very different message from both children's responses. She may interpret the first child as rude and defiant because the child looked the teacher

in the eye. She may interpret the second child's lack of eye contact as appropriately respectful.

There is no way of telling whether the difference in eye contact between the two toddlers was truly cultural or merely individual. That is often the case when one tries to understand if some behavior is cultural or not; however, the teachers' reactions to what they perceived as the children's messages were quite likely cultural. The first teacher expects eye contact on the part of the listener to show that the child is tuned in. The second expects the child to avoid eye contact to show respect for elders who are talking.

When Children Start to Learn Culturally Appropriate Nonverbal Communication

Such lessons start in infancy. During an exercise called "holding babies" that my training partner, Intisar Shareef, and I include in our PITC Training-of-Trainers workshop, a participant explained how babies in her culture start to learn about eye contact. The point of the exercise is to have participants demonstrate different ways to hold babies, which often brings

out interesting cultural information. This person gave a description of holding a baby on a cradle-board. She went on to explain that in her culture it is customary to put a light cloth over the headpiece to cover the baby's eyes. "The idea," she said, "is to teach the baby from the very beginning not to look elders in the eye." The workshop participants were surprised to learn that such cultural lessons start so young!

Another cultural difference that regularly comes out of that exercise has to do with which way the baby faces when being held. Several people demonstrate how they hold the baby toward them so they can see the baby's face and make eye contact. They often say they hold the baby this way so that they can talk to the child. That practice is a contrast to holding the baby with its face and body directed outward so that the child can see *beyond* the adult. Sometimes the people who demonstrate the latter practice make a point of saying how important it is for the baby to get a broader view of the world around her, one that is not focused on the adult alone. Once in a while, someone mentions that paying attention to others keeps the baby from being too focused on herself.

A Contrast in Conversational Styles

The people who hold the baby with his face and body directed outward may be from a culture that is more family- and group-oriented and that prioritizes interdependence over independence. They may be teaching the baby a particular pattern of communication. That lesson in communication is a contrast to the predominant pattern of more independent-minded, individualistic cultures, such as the one Barrera, Corso, and McPherson (2003) call "Euro-American normative culture." Here are examples of those two patterns. The first one involves a European American talking to her friend.

> A mother is deep in adult conversation when her toddler daughter, playing nearby with a basket of toys, comes over to show her mother something she found in the basket. The mother stops talking and turns her attention to the child, commenting on what her daughter is showing her. She then turns back to her friend and resumes the conversation. The child goes back to the basket, but soon comes back to her mother. Again, the mother excuses herself from the adult conversation and gives full attention to the child. A short time later, the child returns with another toy in her hand. The mother ignores her for a bit and then asks the child not to interrupt unless absolutely necessary. When the interruptions continue, the mother makes arrangements to send her daughter to play with the child next door.

Dyadic conversational style. This mother's behavior is probably the result of growing up in a culture where pairs, or *dyad*s, are a common social unit. She gives full attention to her friend and full attention to her daughter, moving from one twosome (or dyad) to another. The child gets a turn for her attention, while the friend waits—and then it is the friend's turn again. The mother finally gives up on what can be thought of as serial dyads and removes the child. In her world, social engagement tends to be a one-on-one affair at least some of the time. Turn-taking in conversations is important.

The dyadic pattern is taught to infants. Going back to this toddler's infancy, we can watch the mother teach turn-taking. The mother talks to her baby daughter from day one. Once her daughter starts babbling, the mother leans over her on the diapering table or wherever she is, making eye contact and responding to the baby's sound. Then she waits, and when the baby makes another sound, the mother responds. This preliminary "conversation" finally led to the way the toddler now communicates with her mother. Barbara Rogoff, an expert in cross-cultural development, would explain the mother–friend–daughter conversation in the previous scenario in anthropological terms. She says, "Middle-class European American social interaction seems to follow a dyadic prototype of one-partner-at-a-time. Even when a group is present, individuals often interact dyadically, treating the group as multiple dyads rather than as an integrated multiparty group" (Rogoff 2003, 144).

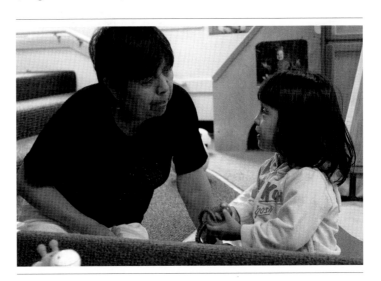

Nondyadic conversational style. Here is another scene in which a parent displays a different communication style when talking with a toddler and an adult. The first scene was from my own experience; the following scenario is from a piece of research. In this scene, a father from an Indian community carries on a conversation with a research assistant while his child, Ramu, plays with a jar containing a ring.

> As the father answered a question from the research assistant, he drew Ramu's attention to the ring inside the jar and demonstrated the series of actions that could be performed with the jar, by opening the lid, rattling the ring inside briefly, then closing the lid again . . . .
>
> When Ramu reached for the jar, his father gave it to him and watched as Ramu began to examine the jar. The father simultaneously continued his conversation with the research assistant.
>
> Ramu took the lid off the jar, took the ring out, and triumphantly showed it to his father, holding it up to his line of vision and smiling happily.
>
> The father nodded, acknowledging what Ramu had accomplished. (Mistry 1993, 111–12, taken from Rogoff [2003]).

The father communicated nonverbally with his child while carrying on a conversation with the research assistant. That is a contrast to the first scene, in which the mother's conversation was a series of dyads. Someone who is used to conversing one-on-one in dyads might decide that the father was not paying enough attention to his child. Although he was not talking, he was communicating. Further, he did it smoothly so that his communication with the child was not an interruption, but it flowed nicely into his conversation with the adult. Teachers who are dyadic, one-on-one conversationalists need to observe other conversational styles. Some adults can talk to children and talk to adults at the same time without anybody becoming frustrated. If you see that happening, it is possible you are observing someone who grew up in a less individualistic culture.

Having different conversational styles does not mean that one's style is right and the other's is wrong. Cultural differences show up in communication, and it is easy to judge negatively whatever does not fit one's own style. Infant care teachers must be willing to examine their feelings of discomfort when confronted with communication styles that are different from their own, rather than regarding those different approaches as wrong or inferior. Discomfort is a good sign—it can mean the infant care teacher is ready to learn something new.

How Children Learn Conversational Styles

Lessons in conversational styles start in infancy, when family members and infant care teachers talk one-on-one with infants—as the workshop participants did in the "holding babies" exercise.

Lessons in the dyadic style are not necessarily universal. Talking directly with infants in intimate, one-on-one interactions is much less common when infants usually experience communication as part of a group. In the nondyadic style, families and infant care teachers may well hold their children facing outward instead of toward them so the babies can observe and hear the same things as adults see and hear. Instead of being apart from the group, the children learn to be participating members of it by not spending much time relating one-on-one with the caring adults (Heath 1983).

A Cultural Difference in Emphasis Between Verbal and Nonverbal Communication

Although children in all cultures learn to talk, in some cultures nonverbal communication is emphasized over verbal communication. When that is the case, infants and toddlers are expected to be good observers and they have many op-

portunities to practice. That expectation may not be as strong in cultures where words are regarded as the main means of communication. Western cultures and others that highly value schooling (which depends on words) are likely to be verbal in many situations. People who regard spoken language as the most important means of communication may be less attentive to subtle messages from nonverbal cues. Those who value nonverbal communication as much as, or more than, words learn to be good observers of others. They attend to what the talkative person may likely miss.

When does the emphasis on nonverbal communication start? Obviously, all cultures use nonverbal communication from the day the child is born. During the first year of a child's life, it is the most effective way to communicate—through touch and body-to-body contact, though sounds can also be effective. In some cultures,

those body-contact messages continue to be the main communication between infant and adult far beyond the first year or so. When babies have body-to-body contact with their mother or infant care teacher most of the day and night, nonverbal communication is enhanced and words become superfluous. Those babies send and receive physical messages 24 hours a day. They are learning a very different kind of communication from babies who are alone in cribs at night and who spend only a part of their waking hours in the arms of adults.

The two communication styles result in differences. For example, anthropologists have observed far less crying in babies who have almost continual body contact compared with those who do not (Rogoff 2003). Babies who experience frequent physical contact give off signals *before* they start to cry, and mothers or infant care teachers often respond to those signals so the babies have no need to signal further. When babies are not in such close contact, crying is a way for them to signal needs. Mothers and infant care teachers depend on those vocal signals, although they may also read the physical signals if they are close by. Crying and verbaliza-

tion become the way to cross the distance between infant and adult.

Babies in both systems learn to communicate their needs, one mostly verbally and one mostly nonverbally. According to Barbara Rogoff, it is important to recognize that some cultural patterns emphasize talk and others depend more on "taciturn engagement that prioritizes silence and perhaps gestures" (2003, 367).

Differences in Perceptions of Infant Learning

In some cultures, learning to be a good observer is more important than communicating with words. Babies who have constant body-to-body contact with an infant care teacher witness a good deal of adult activity that includes nonverbal and verbal communication. These children are part of daily events. That training in observation is good and eventually trains the child to become an active participant in those events. Adults do not necessarily teach children and may not even talk directly to them very much, but they expect children to be paying attention and learning. Learning through observation and participation in a group looks differ-

ent from the way babies learn when the adults express words directly to them in almost every situation. The situations are different, too. Adults who value talking usually speak with babies during caregiving times. They put the babies in appropriate play environments and also talk to them while they are playing. The child-directed talk increases when trained infant care teachers (or educated parents in the United States) know that there is a connection between vocabulary and later school success. In many early childhood programs and in a lot of homes, words are important and are considered a primary source of information.

The questions about cultural differences in communication are many. One such question is, *How can programs help infants and toddlers in their identity formation as cultural beings?* Another related question is, *In what ways can programs help infants and toddlers remain firmly attached to families and home cultures?* Part of the answer involves understanding different communication styles and respecting them. But another question arises: *What role do programs play in preparing infants and toddlers to attend school, where words are of vital importance and communication styles may be different from those of the home?* There are no easy answers to any of those questions, yet all of them are important. The other sections in this guide emphasize "bathing" children in a rich linguistic environment while being responsive to their nonverbal communication and cultural style. I like to imagine a world in which all children gain healthy identities and fit comfortably into their family culture while also learning to move easily in other cultures and succeed in school.

Here is a slightly easier question to answer: *What happens when a child whose family has communication styles related to priorities of interdependence ends up in a program where independence and individuality are main priorities?* Most children and their families experience confusion, at the very least. To minimize difficulties, adults working in these programs need to become conscious of cultural differences. Awareness of different perspectives helps adults to figure out what to do about those differences so that children who are grounded in one system and end up in another one do not experience conflicts that interfere with their growth and development. It is important for infant care teachers and parents to honor and respect each other's differences and to work together to determine what is best for the child.

References

Barrera, Isaura, Rob Corso, and Dianne Macpherson. 2003. *Skilled Dialogue: Strategies for Responding to Cultural Diversity in Early Childhood.* Baltimore, MD: Brookes.

Gleason, Jean Berko, and Nan Bernstein Ratner. 2009. *The Development of Language.* 7th ed. Boston: Pearson/ Allyn & Bacon.

Gonzalez-Mena, Janet. 2008. *Diversity in Early Care and Education: Honoring Differences.* New York: McGraw-Hill, and Washington, DC: National Association for the Education of Young Children.

Greenfield, Patricia M. 1994. "Independence and Interdependence as Developmental Scripts: Implications for Theory, Research, and Practice," in *Cross-Cultural Roots of Minority Child Development.* Edited by P. M. Greenfield and R. R. Cocking, 1–37. Mahwah, NJ: Lawrence Erlbaum.

Heath, Shirley Brice. 1983. *Ways with Words: Language, Life, and Work in Communities and Classrooms.* New York: Cambridge University Press.

Mistry, J. 1993. "Guided Participation in Dhol-Ki-Patti," in *Guided Participation in Cultural Activity by Toddlers and Caregivers.* Edited by B. Rogoff, J. Mistry, A. Goncu, and C. Mosier. *Monographs of the Society for Research in Child Development* 58 (7, Serial no. 236): 102–125.

Rogoff, Barbara. 2003. *The Cultural Nature of Human Development.* New York: Oxford University Press.

Shareef, Intisar, and Janet Gonzalez-Mena. 2008. *Practice in Building Bridges: A Companion Resource to Diversity in Early Care and Education.* 5th ed. Washington, DC: National Association for the Education of Young Children.

Small, Meredith, 1998. Our *Babies, Ourselves: How Biology and Culture Shape the Way We Parent.* New York: Anchor.

Section Six:

Language Development and Literacy

Introduction

*I*n this section, Peter L. Mangione explores links between children's oral language development, particularly vocabulary development, during the infant/toddler years and emergent literacy development throughout the early childhood years. Expressive communication with infants and toddlers is contrasted with business talk. He discusses the relationship basis of early learning of language, the importance of natural, spontaneous communication between infants and nurturing adults, and the impact of adult responsiveness on communication initiated by infants and toddlers. The section closes with an overview of practices that infant care teachers can use to support language development and build a foundation for literacy during the first three years.

Peter L. Mangione is co-director of WestEd's Center for Child and Family Studies. He provides leadership in the development of comprehensive training resources for infant/toddler care teachers, the evaluation of early childhood programs and services, and the creation of resources on learning and curriculum planning for both infant/toddler and preschool programs. His contributions have helped make the Program for Infant/Toddler Care (PITC) a national model for training early childhood practitioners. Mangione received a B.A. in psychology from Oakland University and an M.S. and Ph.D. in education and human development from the University of Rochester. In addition, he studied at the Merrill-Palmer Institute for Child and Family Studies and completed a postdoctoral fellowship at the Max Planck Institute of Psychiatry in Munich, Germany, where he specialized in infant development and the use of video technology to study social interaction.

Building a Foundation for Literacy During the First Three Years

Peter L. Mangione

In the prior section, Janet Gonzalez-Mena imagines "a world in which all children gain healthy identities and fit comfortably into their family culture while also learning to move easily in other cultures and succeed in school." This section explores recent research on children's developing verbal competence and school readiness for literacy development. For many infants and toddlers, the approach to language and communication presented in this section will be a different cultural experience. To be respectful and supportive of cultural experiences at home, infant care teachers

have a dual focus in applying research on oral language and vocabulary development:

- They work to ensure that infants and toddlers feel positive about their developing cultural competence and identity, which are rooted in their experiences at home.
- They attend to the ways infants and toddlers learn in families whose cultures place less emphasis on talking. Children need support from teachers in order to move easily in a culture that places greater emphasis on talking as they continue to develop the ability to communicate in their home culture.

The importance of supporting both language and literacy during the infant/toddler years has received an enormous amount of attention in recent years (Rosenkoetter and Knapp-Philo 2006). Oral language development is related to learning to read at school age, though not as strongly as skills developed at the preschool age, such as alphabet knowledge, phonological awareness, rapid naming of letters and digits, and short-term memory (National Early Literacy Panel 2007). For children from birth to age three, the most promising way to strengthen early literacy is to support oral language development.[1] From the perspective of school readiness,

---

1. The concept of early oral language development, of course, applies to most children, but not children with a severe hearing impairment. This latter group of children would likely follow a different path of language and literacy development.

Lonigan (2003) recommends the following approach to the timing and sequencing of teaching emergent literacy skills and knowledge:

- Literacy programs for young children (up to four years) should focus mainly on improving oral language skills.
- Letter knowledge and phonological sensitivity should be taught explicitly in the preschool and early elementary school period.

As presented in the other sections in this guide, oral language development includes conversational skills, vocabulary development, and communication and language rules, as well as an interest in being read to and hearing stories, rhyming games, finger plays, and songs (Birckmayer, Kennedy, and Stonehouse 2008).

Vocabulary Development

Several leading researchers have suggested that vocabulary development plays a prominent role in emergent literacy and later reading achievement (Snow, Burns, and Griffin 1998; Risley 2005). Hart and Risley's (1995) influential study of early vocabulary development put the spotlight on the relationship of language input and

vocabulary development. They found that the amount or frequency of language spoken to a child was associated with the child's vocabulary production. At thirty-six months of age, children whose parents spoke often to them had vocabularies as high as 700 to 900 words, whereas children whose parents spoke infrequently had vocabularies in the 300 to 500 range. These differences between children in language-rich environments and those in less-rich language environments dramatically increased with age. This research suggests that a high level of early vocabulary input during infancy is the springboard for accelerated vocabulary development through the preschool years.

In a study of maternal language and toddler vocabulary production, Pan et al. (2005) considered both the amount of language and the type of language spoken by mothers. Type of language provided a measure of the variety of words spoken to the child (for example, nouns, verbs, adjectives, prepositions, and pronouns). Pan

et al. (2005) also studied the use of pointing by the mother when communicating. In addition, those researchers examined the influence of different factors on the mother's language use with her child, including her level of education, her verbal language aptitude and literacy, and maternal depression. Pan et al. (2005) found that, at around 24 months, the mother's use of different word types was strongly related to the child's vocabulary production. To a lesser extent, maternal pointing was also related to the child's vocabulary development.

The Pan et al. study (2005) indicated that mothers who spoke frequently were likely to use a variety of language. In addition, those researchers observed that some mothers who used a variety of language when communicating with their children did not necessarily speak frequently. This research suggests that an adult who is talkative with a toddler will naturally provide a variety of language input, but it does not rule out the possibility that an adult with a quiet communication style would also offer a variety of language.

Even though a quiet style may be effective in fostering vocabulary growth, it is recommended that teachers learn to speak frequently or "bathe" children in language. Bathing infants and toddlers in language is likely to offer them experiences with different types of words that promote vocabulary growth and language development.

As stated above, Pan et al. (2005) also examined prior studies (Breznitz and Sherman 1987; Lovejoy et al. 2000) of the link between maternal depression and maternal vocabulary production with toddlers. The Pan et al. study (2005) found that mothers who were depressed or who were experiencing stress talked less to

their children and tended to use a less-varied vocabulary. This study and others suggest that reducing stress on adults by providing emotional support may enhance the adults' communication with young children (Lally and Mangione 2005). Along these lines, the PITC policies of primary care, small groups, and continuity of care may reduce stress on teachers as well as create an intimate setting that facilitates language-rich communication between adults and very young children.

Business Talk

Researchers distinguish two general types of talk that adults use with young children. Risley (2005) refers to one type of communication with infants and toddlers as "business talk" or "here and now" language. Others—for example, Norton (1995–1996)—call this type of language "contextualized." Business talk has to do with managing a present situation or behavior. The focus is on the immediate context, which is why this type of language is called contextualized. An example of business talk is a request, such as asking a child to put blocks away. This type of communication is important. We all depend on business talk in our interactions with children as well as with adults. However, if most of an adult's communication with a child focuses on managing the immediate situation or behavior, the language input is limited. Because business talk is often routine and rudimentary, it alone does not provide young children with a rich variety of language. In contrast, the other general type of language—expressive talk—opens up the world for infants and toddlers.

Expressive Talk

Expressive talk or extra talk has been referred to as "decontextualized" language by others (Norton 1995–1996). Expressive talk adds information and often focuses on the past and future. It moves communication out of the here and now or immediate context; thus it is decontextualized. In fact, one of the most powerful aspects of language is that it allows us to communicate about the past and future. We can describe past experiences, expand on things in the present, and make plans or anticipate what will happen in the future. This type of language becomes meaningful to infants as they gain experience with it. Teachers who frequently use expressive talk often describe objects and actions. They also make comparisons: "The red ball is bigger than the yellow ball." And they ask questions such as "What happened last time?" or "What is going to happen next?" The possibilities with expressive language are endless. Expressive talk enables teachers and young children to create and share meaning.

Positive Relationships and Oral Language Development

Essential for creating shared meaning in social relationships, expressive talk is usually positive, fun, and engaging. When one looks at the number of affirmations a child receives or does not receive, the potential impact of expressive talk on development is dramatic. In an interview, Risley (2005) summarized the following statistical estimates from his research:

- By age four, children whose parents used mostly business talk and little expressive talk heard that they were wrong 250,000 times and that they were right 120,000 times.
- By age four, children whose parents used a moderate amount of business talk and a lot of expressive talk heard that they were wrong 120,000 times and that they were right 750,000 times.

Thus, an emphasis on business talk was associated with more than twice the number of negative messages to the child in the first four years of life. In contrast, frequent expressive talk was related to more than six times as many positive messages to the child by age four.

It is important to note that business talk can be positive, too. Positive examples of business talk include using self-talk to describe one's actions and parallel talk to describe the child's participation during a caregiving routine. Such communication allows the child to follow what is happening in a routine, anticipate what comes next, and participate in the routine. Self-talk and parallel talk during routines can be combined with expressive language; for example, when helping a child to get dressed, a teacher may point to green pants and ask, "Would you like to wear the green pants?" To nurture relationships, teachers make business talk positive and engage in playful, expressive communication with infants and toddlers.

Natural, Spontaneous Communication

In light of the developmental significance of expressive or extra talk, how can teachers make it an integral part of their communication with young children? Risley (2005) suggests that being responsive to a child's interest naturally leads to extra talk. Risley states:

[Capitalize] on the teachable moment to expand and elaborate your child's comment or words. That's where the best teaching happens. It always turns out that's an automatic part of extra talk. It doesn't have to be taught. It's automatically there if you're talking about extra things that are not business.

In a nutshell, Risley observed that the best teaching happens when adults are responsive to children's thoughts and words and communicate in a natural, spontaneous way. As Risley (2005) states: "I don't think it's intentional. We haven't seen any evidence of anybody intentionally doing anything . . . We never saw anybody sitting down and teaching their child anything." Hart and Risley (1995) found that simply talking to young children had a big impact on vocabulary growth.

With infants and toddlers, adults were not intentionally teaching words or giving formal language instruction.

Talking While Interacting with Children

Although Hart and Risley's (1995) research indicated that parents did not intentionally teach children, parents were intentional in their interactions. They were attentive to their children and made comments that elaborated on the children's interests and cues. In Risley's (2005) words:

Talking was laid onto social interaction. . . . Language is laid on that by everybody. In other words, even the most taciturn parents had moments when they were talkative. Their talkativeness had all the features, in terms of positivity and complexity and so on, that the more talkative people had.

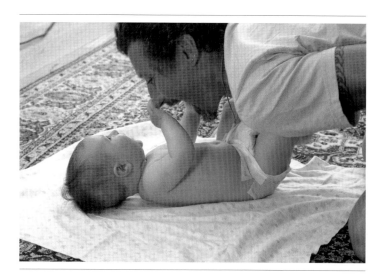

With this comment, Risley makes a crucial point: whether talkative or quiet, everyone has the capability to provide the linguistic complexity an infant or toddler needs. The everyday speech that adults naturally use with infants and toddlers is amply complex—the kind of communication that fosters early language development.

Being Responsive to Children's Communication

Research supports the idea that being responsive with infants sustains interaction. In the language development do-

main, Bloom et al. (1996) reported that, during the language explosion period (around sixteen months to twenty-four months), child-initiated conversations were longer and more complex than adult-initiated conversations. The factor that sustained the rich child-initiated conversations was the adult's responsiveness to the child's communication. Part of sustaining the dance is knowing the child well. In infant/toddler care, the six PITC Essential Policies of primary care provide a context for building a close emotional relationship with a child. Such a relationship opens the door to engaging in increasingly complex dances or interactions with each infant or toddler in child care.

Adding Expressiveness to Responsive Relationships

To foster language and literacy development during the first three years, infant/toddler programs and teachers should focus on the following research-based practices:

(a) Establish enduring relationships with children that foster emotionally positive interactions. The PITC Essential Policies create conditions that lead to the development of close, primary relationships between teachers and children.

(b) Be responsive with infants. The PITC responsive process of Watch-Ask-Adapt is particularly helpful in this regard. (See appendix C, "The Responsive Process.")

(c) Use expressive language in interactions with children to create and share meaning.

The goal of relationship-based care is to meet the child's ever-present need for emotional security, which should be the primary concern of both families and teachers. Attentive, responsive care optimizes all early development, including language development.

The Foundation for Literacy

The development of oral language and vocabulary before age three provides a sturdy foundation for a child. It is important to build on this foundation through the preschool years. For example, in a study of emergent literacy, Lonigan, Burgess, and Anthony (2000) conclude that "significant growth in phonological sensitivity occurs between 3 and 4 years of age." They also report that the skill of connecting sounds to letters does not start to appear until children are in their second year of preschool.

During the infant/toddler age period, rather than trying to teach specific sound-detection skills or letter knowledge—which do not emerge during the first three years—teachers can introduce songs, finger plays, and rhyming games. Such playfulness with language offers to infants and toddlers open-ended experiences with sounds. It is important for infant care teachers to be attentive to the children's responses and to interact with the children responsively.

Strengthening print motivation or infants' and toddlers' interest in print has also been found to have an influence on literacy development. Interest in print during the infant/toddler years can be encouraged in numerous ways. Throughout infancy, a responsive approach is recommended with books and print. To sustain children's interest, teachers follow the children's lead. In the DVD *Early Messages: Facilitating Language Development and Communication* (PITC 1998), Kathleen McCartney vividly conveys this message:

Infants love books. And they are very likely to pull one off a shelf and bring it over to a caregiver. But what they want to do with the book might not always correspond directly with what a caregiver thinks should be done with a book. What we think is that you open it up, you start at the beginning, you turn the page, and you read what's on the page. An infant might want to start at the back. They might actually want to chomp on the book a little bit, or they might want to just look at the pictures and they might want to just point and have things labeled to them. So, what I tell caregivers who are working with infants and very young toddlers is to follow their lead. They'll let you know what they want to do with the book. And I don't think we have to be rigid in terms of "We're going to read what's on the printed page no matter what it is." Instead, the book can be used as an object that the young infant is going to explore, just like any other object.

For infants and toddlers, a first step in building interest about anything, including books, is exploration. McCartney's suggestion to let infants and toddlers freely explore books allows teachers to observe the children's interests and follow their lead.

For older toddlers, a technique called Dialogic Reading may be appropriate. Use of this technique depends on the child's ability to engage in an activity that requires joint attention. Lonigan (2003) summarizes Dialogic Reading as the type of help provided to the child:

- Focuses on the skills already scaffolded (built up through previous interactions)
- Builds on previous readings of the book
- Follows the child's interest both within a book and in choice of books

Once again, the emphasis is on being responsive—starting with what the child already knows and then following the child's interest.

Facilitating Language and Literacy Development

The DVD *Early Messages* (PITC 1998) presents a responsive approach to early language and literacy development. The DVD centers on four key points and recommends 10 strategies to facilitate infants' language and literacy development. The key points link language development to the broader context of early development:

- Acquiring language is complex. It is not taught. Infants play an active role in learning language.
- Under typical circumstances, infants learn language. Experience with communication and language is key.
- Language development varies from individual to individual and from cultural context to cultural context.

- Infants learn language within human relationships. Experience with language typically occurs during everyday routines/activities.

The first two points remind us that infants and toddlers play an active role in their learning and that input from adults is essential in order for them to learn. Of course, the manner in which adults provide language input is crucial. As stated earlier, rather than direct teaching, research supports a responsive approach with infants—one in which the adult follows the lead of the active learner and enhances the experience based on the child's interests. In addition, there are multiple paths to acquiring language. Teachers need to be responsive and attuned to individual and cultural differences in children's experiences with language. Finally, attunement grows from a close, enduring relationship with a child. The everyday experiences teachers create and share with infants have a profound impact on children. Infants and toddlers will prosper if they are in relationships with teachers who make language a positive and engaging part of those relationships.

The 10 strategies presented in *Early Messages* (PITC 1998) are listed in Table 1. These strategies offer specific practices that teachers can use to facilitate overall language development, including vocabulary development and interest in literacy. Taken together, they represent a broad-based approach to facilitating early language development, which provides the foundation for learning to read in elementary school.

Supporting Bilingual Development

Many children entering infant/toddler care come from families with a home language other than English. The responsive approach presented throughout this guide applies to infants who are learning more than one language. Section Four, in particular, addresses bilingual development. In addition, one of the 10 strategies in *Early Messages* (PITC 1998) specifically focuses on supporting bilingual development. The general recommendation is that teachers need to support the development of competence in each language the child is acquiring, both at home and in the group care setting.

The Child's Whole Experience

Finally, every experience an infant or toddler has is a whole experience—at first the child's experiences are undifferentiated and, as the child develops, they become increasingly integrated. In other words, the way the infant experiences the world moves from everything being merged together to distinct concepts being connected together. Teachers can best sustain and foster a child's evolving sense of wholeness or coherence by providing the child with a stable, responsive relationship. And teachers can greatly enhance this development by making language—and literacy—a natural, positive part of every relationship they create with an infant or toddler.

Table 1
Strategies for Supporting Language Development

Be responsive when children initiate communication.

Engage in nonverbal communication.

Use child-directed language.

Use self-talk and parallel talk.

Help children expand language.

Support bilingual development.

Attend to individual development and needs.

Engage infants with books and stories.

Be playful with language.

Create a communication-friendly environment.

Source: PITC 1998.

References

Birckmayer, J., A. Kennedy, and A. Stonehouse. 2008. *From Lullabies to Literature: Stories in the Lives of Infants and Toddlers.* Washington, DC: National Association for the Education of Young Children.

Bloom, L., C. Marquis, E. Tinker, and N. Fujita. 1996. "Early Conversations and Word Learning: Contributions from Child and Adult," *Child Development* 67:3135–153.

Breznitz, Z., and T. Sherman. 1987. "Speech Patterning of Natural Discourse of Well and Depressed Mothers and Their Young Children," *Child Development* 76:395–400.

California Department of Education. 2007. *Infant/Toddler Learning & Development Program Guidelines.* Sacramento: California Department of Education.

Hart, B., and T. R. Risley. 1995. *Meaningful Differences in the Everyday Experience of Young American Children.* Baltimore, MD: Brookes.

Lally, J. R., and P. L. Mangione. 2005. "Policy Recommendations to Support Early Language and Literacy Experiences in the Home and in Child Care," in *Learning to Read the World: Language and Literacy in the First Three Years.* Edited by S. Rosenkoetter and J. Knapp. Washington, DC. Teaching Strategies Press.

Lonigan, C. J. 2003. Children's Emergent Literacy and Family Literacy. Unpublished manuscript, Florida State University.

Lonigan, C. J., S. R. Burgess, and J. L. Anthony. 2000. "Development of Emergent Literacy and Early Reading Skills in Preschool Children: Evidence from a Latent-Variable Longitudinal Study," *Developmental Psychology* 36 (5):596–613.

Lovejoy, M. C., P. A. Graczyk, E. O'Hare, and G. Newman. 2000. "Maternal Depression and Parenting Behavior," *Clinical Psychology Review* 20:561–92.

National Early Literacy Panel. 2007. *Synthesizing the Scientific Research on Development of Early Literacy in Young Children.* Washington, DC: National Institute for Literacy.

Norton, D. G. 1995–1996. "Early Linguistic Interaction and School Achievement: An Ethnographical, Ecological Perspective," *Zero to Three* 16 (December 1995/January 1996):8–14.

Pan, B. A., M. L. Rowe, D. S. Singer, and C. E. Snow. 2005. "Maternal Correlates of Growth in Toddler Vocabulary Production in Low-Income Families," *Child Development* 76 (4):763–82.

PITC (Program for Infant/Toddler Care). 1998. *Early Messages: Facilitating Language Development and Communication.* DVD. Sacramento: California Department of Education.

Risley, T. 2005. http://www.childrenofthecode.org/interviews/risley.htm.

Rosenkoetter, S. E., and J. Knapp-Philo, eds. 2006. *Learning to Read the World: Language and Literacy in the First Three Years.* Washington, DC: Zero to Three Press.

Siegal, D. J. 1999. *The Developing Mind.* New York: The Guilford Press.

Snow, C. E., S. Burns, and P. Griffin. 1998. *Preventing Reading Difficulties in Young Children.* Washington, DC: National Academies Press.

Appendixes

Appendix A

California Infant/Toddler Learning & Development Foundations

Language Development

"The acquisition of language and speech seems deceptively simple. Young children learn their mother tongue rapidly and effortlessly, from babbling at six months of age to full sentences by the end of three years, and follow the same developmental path regardless of culture." (Kuhl 2004, 831)

As is true of human development in infancy overall, language development occurs in the context of relationships. Emotion and language development in the early years are linked, as "much of the form and content of communication between infants and their caregivers in the first year of life depends upon affective expression" (Bloom and Capatides 1987, 1513). The relationship basis of early language development appears right at the beginning of life. Newborns prefer the sounds of their mothers' voices (De-Casper and Fifer 1980). They also prefer the language spoken by their mother during her pregnancy (Moon, Cooper, and Fifer 1993).

Adults typically modify their speech when communicating with young infants. Research suggests that infant-directed speech (also referred to as "parentese" or "motherese") has qualities, notably its pitch or prosody, that distinguish it from adult-directed speech (Cooper and others 1997). Preverbal infants communicate through eye contact, facial expressions, gestures, and sounds. Understanding language precedes speaking it (Bloom and others 1996). In addition, before being able to use language effectively, infants demonstrate that they have gained some understanding of the social processes involved in communication through engaging in turn-taking behavior in proto-conversations with their parents or infant care teachers.

There is broad variability in language development in its pattern and pace (Bloom and Capatides 1987). However, the process of early language development is fundamentally the same across cultures and languages. In describing early language development, Kuhl (2002, 115) states: "One of the puzzles in language development is to explain the orderly transition that all infants go through during development. Infants the world over achieve certain milestones in linguistic development at roughly the same time, regardless of the language they are exposed to."

Perceptual processes play an important role in language development. As Gogate, Walker-Andrews, and Bahrick (2001, 13) note: "A diverse set of experimental findings suggests that early lexical comprehension owes much to infants' developing ability to perceive intersensory relations in auditory-visual events," [for example, speech]. Experience also affects language development from very early in life. One of the ways experience influences language development is through its impact on perception early in infancy. Prior to infants' first spoken words, or word comprehension, they have already "come to recognize the perceptual properties of their native language" (Kuhl 2002, 119). Infants are learning about the prosodic or sound characteristics of their native language: by nine months of age, English-speaking infants demonstrate a preference for the prosodic stress pattern characteristic of words in the English language (Jusczyk, Cutler, and Redanz 1993). Kuhl (2002, 112) concludes: "At age one—prior to the time infants begin to master higher levels of language, such as sound-meaning correspondences, contrastive phonology, and grammatical rules—infants' perceptual and perceptual-motor systems have been altered by linguistic experience. Phonetic perception has changed dramatically to conform to the native-language pattern, and language-specific speech production has emerged."

Receptive Language

Infants excel at detecting patterns in spoken language (Kuhl 2000). The literature indicates that infants' speech perception abilities are strong. Not only do infants understand more vocabulary than they are able to produce, but they also demonstrate awareness of the properties of the language or languages they are exposed to before they acquire words (Ingram 1999). During the first six months of life, infants are better than adults at perceiving various types of contrasts in speech (Plunkett and Schafer 1999). Infants improve in their ability to discriminate the sounds characteristic of their native language, while losing their abilities to discriminate some sounds characteristic of languages other than

their native language (Cheour and others 1998). According to Kuhl (2004), the idea of "neural commitment" explains the process of language acquisition within a social and biological context. According to this view, from early infancy young children use a mental filter to orient with greater efficiency and accuracy to the speech sounds characteristic of their native language. This strategy enables infants to identify the phonemic units most useful to them in their native language, as a building block to later word acquisition (Kuhl 2004).

Expressive Language

Infants use their expressive language skills to make sounds or use gestures or speech to begin to communicate. Even pre-verbal infants use vocalizing or babbling to express themselves. They also imitate the sounds and rhythm of adult speech. As they develop, infants generate increasingly understandable sounds or verbal communication. They demonstrate their expressive language abilities through asking questions and responding to questions, and through their repetition of sounds or rhymes. Children typically acquire their first 50 words between the ages of one and two (Ingram 1999). Kuczaj (1999, 145) notes: "The 24-month-old child with a productive vocabulary between 50 and 600 words will easily quadruple or quintuple her vocabulary in the next year, and then add between 3000 and 4000 words per year to her productive vocabulary until she graduates from high school."

Infants' use of nonverbal gestures as a form of communication appears to be a typical feature of early language development, although there is considerable variability among children (Acredolo and Goodwyn 1988). The use of communicative gestures appears to generally precede the child's first words (Carpenter, Nagell, and Tomasello 1998). Commenting on the infant's motivation to use gestures, Acredolo and Goodwyn (1997, 30) state: "There is something very special about the human infant's capacity to communicate with gestures. In fact, normal infants seem so intent on communicating once they realized there's somebody out there 'listening,' that they find creative ways to do so before they have mastered words."

Communication Skills and Knowledge

Sensitivity to the timing of conversational exchanges has been demonstrated through research on proto-conversations involving young infants (Rochat, Querido, and Striano 1999). Infants use speech, gestures, and facial expressions as well direct their attention to communicate to others. As they grow, they increasingly understand the rules or conventions of social communication and the communication of others, and benefit from an expanded vocabulary that helps them express themselves through words. As they develop, infants gain experience in communicating with both peers and adults, very different conversational partners. According to Pan and Snow (1999, 231): "interaction with peers, who are less competent and usually less cooperative partners than adults, requires use of more sophisticated conversational skills, such

as knowing how and when to interrupt, how to remedy overlaps and interruptions by others, and how to make topic-relevant moves." It is noteworthy that the child care setting typically offers abundant opportunities for communication with both adult and child conversational partners.

Interest in Print

Infants show an interest in print at first through physically exploring books through mouthing or handling, and through focusing on print in the environment around them. Turning the pages of books, looking at books or pictures, asking for a favorite book or telling a favorite story with an adult are other indicators of interest in print. As infants grow older, making intentional marks on paper with a crayon or marker, pretending to read, pretending to write, repeating stories, repeating rhymes, recognizing images in books, noticing common symbols and words, and enjoying books are all related to interest in print. Interest in print can be considered one aspect of emergent literacy, the idea that literacy develops from early childhood, rather than being something that only becomes relevant upon school entry (Whitehurst Lonigan 1998). Because early experiences with print contribute to later literacy, shared book reading is recommended as a valuable way to promote emergent literacy (Whitehurst and Lonigan 1998).

Foundation: Receptive Language

The developing ability to understand words and increasingly complex utterances

8 months	18 months	36 months
At around eight months of age, children show understanding of a small number of familiar words and react to the infant care teacher's overall tone of voice.	At around 18 months of age, children show understanding of one-step requests that have to do with the current situation.	At around 36 months of age, children demonstrate understanding of the meaning of others' comments, questions, requests, or stories. (By 36 mos.; American Academy of Pediatrics 2004, 307)
For example, the child may:	**For example, the child may:**	**For example, the child may:**
• Smile and look toward the door when the infant care teacher says, "Daddy's here." (Scaled score of 10 for 7:16–8:15 mos.; Bayley 2006, 87) • Wave arms and kick legs in excitement when the infant care teacher says, "bottle." (8 mos.; Meisels and others 2003, 18) • Smile when the infant care teacher uses baby talk and make a worried face when she uses a stern voice. (8 mos.; Meisels and others 2003, 18; by end of 7 mos.; American Academy of Pediatrics 2004)	• Go to the cubby when the infant care teacher says that it is time to put on coats to go outside. (Scaled score of 10 for 17:16 to 18:15 mos.; Bayley 2006, 90; 12–18 mos.; Lerner and Ciervo 2003; 12 mos.; Coplan 1993, 2; by 24 mos.; American Academy of Pediatrics 2004; 12 mos.; Coplan 1993, 2; 24 mos.; Meisels and others 2003, 46) • Cover up the doll when the infant care teacher says, "Cover the baby with the blanket." (Scaled score of 10 for 17:16–18:15 mos.; Bayley 2006, 90; 12–18 mos.; Lerner and Ciervo 2003; 12 mos.; Coplan 1993, 2; by 24 mos.; American Academy of Pediatrics 2004) • Go to the sink when the infant care teacher says that it is time to wash hands. (Scaled score of 10 for 17:16–18:15 mos.; Bayley 2006, 90; 12–18 mos.; Lerner and Ciervo 2003; 12 mos.; Coplan 1993, 2; by 24 mos.; American Academy of Pediatrics 2004; 24 mos.; Meisels and others 2003, 46) • Get a tissue when the infant care teacher says, "Please go get a tissue. We need to wipe your nose." (18 mos.; Meisels and others 2003, 36)	• Look for a stuffed bear when the infant care teacher asks, "Where's your bear?" (24–36 mos.; Coplan 1993, 2–3; scaled score of 10 for 34:16–35:15; Bayley 2006) • Get the bin of blocks when the infant care teacher asks what the child wants to play with. (24–36 mos.; Coplan 1993, 2–3; scaled score of 10 for 34:16–35:15; Bayley 2006) • Show understanding of words such as *no, not,* and *don't,* and utterances such as when the infant care teacher says, "There's no more milk," or "Those don't go there." (24–36 mos.; Parks 2004, p. 99) • Know the names of most objects in the immediate environment. (By 36 mos.; American Academy of Pediatrics 2004) • Understand requests that include simple prepositions, such as, "Please put your cup on the table," or "Please get your blanket out of your backpack." (By 36 mos.; Coplan 1993, 2; by 36 mos.; American Academy of Pediatrics 2004; 24–27 mos.; Parks 2004, 97) • Laugh when an adult tells a silly joke or makes up rhymes with nonsense "words." (By 36 mos.; American Academy of Pediatrics 2004, 307) • Show understanding of the meaning of a story by laughing at the funny parts or by asking questions. (By 36 mos.; American Academy of Pediatrics 2004, 307)

Chart continues on next page.

Receptive Language

Behaviors leading up to the foundation (4 to 7 months)	Behaviors leading up to the foundation (9 to 17 months)	Behaviors leading up to the foundation (19 to 35 months)
During this period, the child may: • Vocalize in response to the infant care teacher's speech. (3–6 mos.; Parks 2004) • Quiet down when hearing the infant care teacher's voice. (3–6 mos.; Parks 2004) • Turn toward the window when hearing a fire truck drive by. (4–6 mos.; Coplan 1993, 2) • Quiet down and focus on the infant care teacher as he talks to the child during a diaper change. (4 mos.; Meisels and others 2003, 10) • Look at or turn toward the infant care teacher who says the child's name. (Mean for 5 mos.; Bayley 2006, 86; by 7 mos.; American Academy of Pediatrics 2004, 209; 9 mos.; Coplan 1993, 2; 12 mos.; Meisels and others 2003, 27; 5–7 mos.; Parks 2004)	During this period, the child may: • Follow one-step simple requests if the infant care teacher also uses a gesture to match the verbal request, such as pointing to the blanket when asking the child to get it. (9 mos.; Coplan 1993, 2) • Look up and momentarily stop reaching into the mother's purse when she says "no no." (9–12 mos.; Parks 2004, 95) • Show understanding of the names for most familiar objects and people. (Scaled score of 10 for 16:16–17:15 mos.; Bayley 2006, 90; 8–12 mos.; Parks 2004, 94)	During this period, the child may: • Show understanding of pronouns, such as *he, she, you, me, I,* and *it;* for example, by touching own nose when the infant care teacher says, "Where's your nose?" and then touching the infant care teacher's nose when he says, "And where's my nose?" (19 mos.; Hart and Risley 1999, 61; 20–24 mos.; Parks 2004, 96) • Follow two-step requests about unrelated events, such as, "Put the blocks away and then go pick out a book." (24 mos.; Coplan 1993, 2; by 24 mos.; American Academy of Pediatrics 2004, 270; 24–29 mos.; Parks 2004, 104; three-part command by 36 mos.; American Academy of Pediatrics 2004, 307) • Answer adults' questions; for example, communicate "apple" when a parent asks what the child had for snack. (28 mos.; Hart and Risley 1999, 95)

Foundation: Expressive Language

The developing ability to produce the sounds of language and use vocabulary and increasingly complex utterances

8 months	18 months	36 months
At around eight months of age, children experiment with sounds, practice making sounds, and use sounds or gestures to communicate needs, wants, or interests.	At around 18 months of age, children say a few words and use conventional gestures to tell others about their needs, wants, and interests. (By 15 to 18 mos.; American Academy of Pediatrics 2004 270; Coplan 1993, 1; Hulit and Howard 2006, 142)	At around 36 months of age, children communicate in a way that is understandable to most adults who speak the same language they do. Children combine words into simple sentences and demonstrate the ability to follow some grammatical rules of the home language. (By 36 mos.; American Academy of Pediatrics 2004, 307; 30–36 mos.; Parks 2004; 24–36 mos.; Lerner and Ciervo 2003; by 36 mos.; Hart and Risley 1999, 67)
For example, the child may:	**For example, the child may:**	**For example, the child may:**
• Vocalize to get the infant care teacher's attention. (6.5–8 mos.; Parks 2004) • Repeat sounds when babbling, such as "da da da da" or "ba ba ba ba." (By 7 mos.; American Academy of Pediatrics 2004, 209; 6–7 mos.; Hulit and Howard 2006, 122; scaled score of 10 for 7:16–8:15 on Bayley 2006, 106; 4–6.5 mos.; Parks 2004; 6 mos.; Locke 1993) • Wave to the infant care teacher when he waves and says, "bye-bye" as he leaves for his break. (6–9 mos.; Parks 2004, 121) • Lift arms to the infant care teacher to communicate a desire to be held. (7–9 mos.; Coplan 1993, 3; 5–9 mos.; Parks 2004, 121)	• Look at a plate of crackers, then at the infant care teacher, and communicate "more." (Scaled score of 10 for 16:16–17:15; Bayley 2006; 14–20 mos.; Parks 2004) • Point to an airplane in the sky and look at the infant care teacher. (17.5–18.5 mos.; Parks 2004, 123) • Use the same word to refer to similar things, such as "milk" while indicating the pitcher, even though it is filled with juice. (18 mos.; Meisels and others 2003, p. 37) • Use two words together, such as "Daddy give." (18 mos.; National Research Council and Institute of Medicine 2000, 127) • Shake head "no" when offered more food. (18 mos.; Meisels and others 2003, 37) • Jabber a string of sounds into the toy telephone. (18 mos.; Meisels and others 2003, 37) • Gesture "all gone" by twisting wrists to turn hands up and down when finished eating lunch. (12–19 mos.; Parks 2004, 122) • Use made-up "words" to refer to objects or experiences that only familiar adults will know the meaning of; for example "wo-wo" when wanting to go next door to visit the puppy. (12–22 mos.; Hulit and Howard 2006, p. 130)	• Use the past tense, though not always correctly; for example, "Daddy goed to work," "She falled down." (27–30 mos.; Hulit and Howard 2006, 182; 30–36 mos.; Parks 2004; 28 mos.; Hart and Risley 1999, 95 and 129–30) • Use the possessive, though not always correctly; for example, "That's you car" or "Her Megan." (Scaled score of 10 for 34:16–35:15; Bayley 2006) • Use a few prepositions, such as "on" the table. (33-35.5 mos.; Parks 2004, p. 116) • Talk about what she will do in the future, such as "I gonna get a kitty." (33–36 mos.; Hart and Risley 1999, 131) • Use 300–1000 words. (35+ mos.; Parks 2004, 116) • Use the plural form of nouns, though not always correctly; for example, "mans," and "mouses." (By 36 mos.; American Academy of Pediatrics 2004, 307; 28 mos.; Hart and Risley 1999, 95) • Express, "Uncle is coming to pick me up." (36 mos.; Hoff 2005)

Chart continues on next page.

Expressive Language

Behaviors leading up to the foundation (4 to 7 months)	Behaviors leading up to the foundation (9 to 17 months)	Behaviors leading up to the foundation (19 to 35 months)
During this period, the child may: • Squeal when excited. (5 mos.; Lerner and Ciervo 2003; by 7 mos.; American Academy of Pediatrics 2004, 209) • Make an angry noise when another child takes a toy. (5–6 mos.; Parks 2004) • Make a face of disgust to tell the infant care teacher that she does not want any more food. (6–9 mos.; Lerner and Ciervo 2003)	During this period, the child may: • Babble using the sounds of his home language. (6–10 mos.; Cheour and others 1998) • Consistently use utterances to refer to favorite objects or experiences that only familiar adults know the meaning of; for example, "ba ba ba ba" for blanket. (9 mos.; Bates, Camaioni, and Volterra 1975; 12 mos.; Coplan 1993, 3; 12 mos.; Davies 2004, 166; 9–10 mos.; Hulit and Howard 2006, 123) • Express "Mama" or "Dada" when the mother or father, respectively, enters the room. (10 mos.; Coplan 1993, 1) • Say a first word clearly enough that the infant care teacher can understand the word within the context; for example, "gih" for give, "see," "dis" for this, "cookie," "doggie," "uh oh" and "no." (Mean age 11 mos.; Hart and Risley 1999, 56) • Name a few familiar favorite objects. (Around 12 mos.; Coplan 1993, 3; mean age 13 mos., range 9–16 mos.; Hulit and Howard 2006, 132; between 10 and 15 mos.; National Research Council and Institute of Medicine 2000, 127) • Change tone when babbling, so that the child's babbles sound more and more like adult speech. (By 12 mos.; American Academy of Pediatrics 2004; 7.5–12 mos.; Parks, 2004; 7–8 mos.; Hulit and Howard 2006, 123) • Use expressions; for example, "uh oh" when milk spills or when something falls off the table. (12.5–14.5 mos.; Parks 2004) • Say "up" and lift arms to be picked up by the infant care teacher. (Scaled score of 9 for 16:16–17:15 mos.; Bayley 2006, 108; 12–14 mos.; Parks 2004, 132)	During this period, the child may: • Tend to communicate about objects, actions, and events that are in the here and now. (12–22 mos.; Hulit and Howard 2006, 141) • Use some words to refer to more than one thing; for example, "night-night" to refer to bedtime or to describe darkness. (12–22 mos.; Hulit and Howard 2006, 132) • Use many new words each day. (18–20 mos.; Coplan, 1993, 1; 18–24 mos.; Hulit and Howard 2006, 137) • Begin to combine a few words into mini-sentences to express wants, needs, or interests; for example, "more milk," "big doggie," "no night-night" or "go bye-bye." (18–20 mos.; Coplan 1993, 1; 24 mos.; Meisels and others 2003, 47; by 24 mos.; American Academy of Pediatrics 2004, 270; 18–24 mos.; Hulit and Howard 2006, 143; scaled score of 10 for 32:16–33:15; Bayley 2006, 114; 20.5–24 mos.; Parks 2004, 133) • Have a vocabulary of about 80 words. (19 mos.; Hart and Risley 1999, 61) • Start adding articles before nouns, such as, "a book" or "the cup." (20 mos.; Hart and Risley 1999, 63) • Use own name when referring to self. (18-24 mos.; Parks 2004) • Ask questions with raised intonations at the end, such as "Doggy go?" (22–26 mos.; Hulit and Howard 2006, 144) • Communicate using sentences of three to five words, such as "Daddy go store?" or "Want more rice." (30 mos.; Coplan 1993, 1; 25 mos.; Hart and Risley 1999, 63)

Foundation: Communication Skills and Knowledge

The developing ability to communicate nonverbally and verbally

8 months	18 months	36 months
At around eight months of age, children participate in back-and-forth communication and games.	At around 18 months of age, children use conventional gestures and words to communicate meaning in short back-and-forth interactions and use the basic rules of conversational turn-taking when communicating. (Bloom, Rocissano, and Hood 1976)	At around 36 months of age, children engage in back-and-forth conversations that contain a number of turns, with each turn building upon what was said in the previous turn. (Hart and Risley 1999, 122)
For example, the child may:	**For example, the child may:**	**For example, the child may:**
• Put arms up above head when the infant care teacher says, "soooo big." (8 mos.; Meisels and others 2003, 19) • Try to get the infant care teacher to play peek-a-boo by hiding her face behind a blanket, uncovering her face, and laughing. (8 mos.; Meisels and others 2003, 19) • Pull the infant care teacher's hands away from his face during a game of peek-a-boo. (Scaled score of 11 for 7:16–8:15 mos.; Bayley 2006, 106) • Try to clap hands to get the infant care teacher to continue playing pat-a-cake. (8 mos.; Meisels and others 2003, 19) • Make sounds when the infant care teacher is singing a song. (8 mos.; Meisels and others 2003, 19) • Interact with the infant care teacher while singing a song with actions or while doing finger plays. (Scaled score of 11 for 8:16–9:15 mos.; Bayley 2006)	• Respond to the infant care teacher's initiation of conversation through vocalizations or nonverbal communication. (12–19 mos.; Hart and Risley 1999, 37) • Initiate interactions with the infant care teacher by touching, vocalizing, or offering a toy. (12–19 mos.; Hart and Risley 1999, 37) • Jabber into a toy phone and then pause, as if to listen to someone on the other end. (18 mos.; Meisels and others 2003, 37) • Shake head or express "no" when the infant care teacher asks if the child is ready to go back inside. (18 mos.; Meisels and others 2003, 37) • Respond to the infant care teacher's comment about a toy with an additional, but related, action or comment about the same toy; for example, make a barking sound when the infant care teacher pats a toy dog and says, "Nice doggie." (By 18 mos.; Bloom, Rocissano, and Hood 1976)	• Persist in trying to get the infant care teacher to respond by repeating, speaking more loudly, expanding on what the child said, or touching the infant care teacher. (After 30 mos.; Hart and Risley 1999, 38) • Repeat part of what the adult just said in order to continue the conversation. (31–34 mos.; Hulit and Howard 2006, 186; by 24 mos.; American Academy of Pediatrics 2004) • Make comments in a conversation that the other person has difficulty understanding; for example, suddenly switch topics or use pronouns without making clear what is being talked about. (31–34 mos.; Hulit and Howard 2006, 192) • Answer adults' questions, such as "What's that?" and "Where did it go?" (31–34 mos.; Hulit and Howard 2006, 185; 24–36 mos.; Parks 2004) • Begin to create understandable topics for a conversation partner. • Sometimes get frustrated if the infant care teacher does not understand what the child is trying to communicate. (28.5–36 mos.; Parks 2004, 129) • Participate in back-and-forth interaction with the infant care teacher by speaking, giving feedback, and adding to what was originally said. (29–36 mos.; Hart and Risley 1999, 36, 39–40)

Chart continues on next page.

Communication Skills and Knowledge

Behaviors leading up to the foundation (4 to 7 months)	Behaviors leading up to the foundation (9 to 17 months)	Behaviors leading up to the foundation (19 to 35 months)
During this period, the child may:	During this period, the child may:	During this period, the child may:
• Respond with babbling when the infant care teacher asks a question. (Hart and Risley 1999, 55)	• Copy the infant care teacher in waving "bye-bye" to a parent as he leaves the room. (Scaled score of 9 for 12:16–13:15 mos.; Bayley 2006, No. 14, 88; 8 mos.; Meisels and others 2003, 19)	• Ask and answer simple questions, such as "What's that?" (19 mos.; Hart and Risley 1999, 61)
• Laugh when a parent nuzzles her face in the child's belly, vocalizes expectantly when she pulls back, and laugh when she nuzzles again. (3–6 mos.; Parks 2004, 11)	• Purse lips after hearing and seeing the infant care teacher make a sputtering sound with her lips. (9 mos.; Apfel and Provence 2001)	• Say, "huh?" when interacting with the infant care teacher to keep interaction going. (19 mos.; Hart and Risley 1999, 62)
• Move body in a rocking motion to get the infant care teacher to continue rocking. (4-5 mos.; Parks 2004, 57)	• Repeat the last word in an adult's question in order to continue the conversation; for example, saying "dat" after the infant care teacher asks, "What is that?" (11–16 mos.; Hart and Risley 1999, 83)	• Repeat or add on to what she just said if the infant care teacher does not respond right away. (20–28 mos.; Hart and Risley 1999, 105)
• Babble back and forth with the infant care teacher during diaper change. (5.5–6.5 mos.; Parks 2004, 125)	• Respond with "yes" or "no" when asked a simple question. (11–16 mos.; Hart and Risley 1999, 83)	• Engage in short back-and-forth interactions with a family member by responding to comments, questions, and prompts. (20–28 mos.; Hart and Risley 1999, 39)
	• Hold out a toy for the infant care teacher to take and then reach out to accept it when the infant care teacher offers it back. (12–15 mos.; Parks 2004, 122)	• Respond almost immediately after a parent finishes talking in order to continue the interaction. (20–28 mos.; Hart and Risley 1999, 97)
	• Show an understanding that a conversation must build on what the other partner says; for example, expressing, "bear" when the infant care teacher points to the stuffed bear and asks, "What's that?" (16 mos.; Hart and Risley 1999, 81)	• Get frustrated if the infant care teacher does not understand what the child is trying to communicate. (24–28.5 mos.; Parks 2004)
	• Initiate back-and-forth interaction with the infant care teacher by babbling and then waiting for the infant care teacher to respond before babbling again. (11–19 mos.; Hart and Risley 1999, 77; 12 mos.; Meisels and others 2003, 27)	• Attempt to continue conversation, even when the adult does not understand him right away, by trying to use different words to communicate the meaning. (27–30 mos.; Hulit and Howard 2006, 182)
	• Say "mmm" when eating, after a parent says, "mmm." (11–19 mos.; Hart and Risley 1999, 78)	• Sustain conversation about one topic for one or two turns, usually about something that is in the here and now. (20–28 mos.; Hart and Risley 1999, 107; 27–30 mos.; Hulit and Howard 2006, 182)
		• Respond verbally to adults' questions or comments. (27–30 mos.; Hulit and Howard 2006, 182)

Foundation: Interest in Print

The developing interest in engaging with print
in books and in the environment

8 months	18 months	36 months
At around eight months of age, children explore books and show interest in adult-initiated literacy activities, such as looking at photos and exploring books together with an adult. (Scaled score of 10 for 7:16–8:15 mos.; Bayley 2006, 57; infants; National Research Council 1999, 28)	At around 18 months of age, children listen to the adult and participate while being read to by pointing, turning pages, or making one- or two-word comments. Children actively notice print in the environment.	At around 36 months of age, children show appreciation for books and initiate literacy activities: listening, asking questions, or making comments while being read to; looking at books on their own; or making scribble marks on paper and pretending to read what is written. (Schickedanz and Casbergue 2004, 11)
For example, the child may:	**For example, the child may:**	**For example, the child may:**
• Point to or indicate an object that he would like the infant care teacher to pay attention to. • Look intently at photographs of classmates when the infant care teacher talks about the pictures. (8–9 mos.; Parks 2004, 71) • Look at pictures that a parent points to while reading a storybook. (Scaled score of 10 for 7:16–8:15 mos.; Bayley 2006, 57; infants; National Research Council 1999, 28) • Hold a book and try to turn the pages. (Scaled score of 10 for 7:16–8:15 mos.; Bayley 2006, 57)	• Attempt to turn the pages of a paper book, sometimes turning more than one page at a time. (15–18 mos.; Parks 2004) • Pretend to read the back of a cereal box while sitting at the kitchen table in the house area. (15–18 mos.; Parks 2004, 27) • Recognize a favorite book by its cover. (Toddler; National Research Council 1999, 28) • Pull the infant care teacher by the hand to the bookshelf, point, and express "book" to get the infant care teacher to read a story. (12–18 mos.; Lerner and Ciervo 2003) • Point to or indicate a familiar sign in the neighborhood.	• Enjoy both being read to and looking at books by himself. (30–36 mos.; Parks 2004) • Pretend to read books to stuffed animals by telling a story that is related to the pictures and turning the book around to show the picture to the stuffed animals, just as the infant care teacher does when reading to a small group of children. (Ehri and Sweet 1991, 199; 24–36 mos.; Sulzby 1985) • Talk about the trip to the library and ask about the next trip. (35 mos.; Hart and Risley 1999, 128) • Recite much of a favorite book from memory while "reading" it to others or self. (36 mos.; National Research Council 1999, 28) • Try to be careful with books. (By 36 mos.; National Research Council 1999, 3)

Chart continues on next page.

Interest in Print

Behaviors leading up to the foundation (4 to 7 months)	Behaviors leading up to the foundation (9 to 17 months)	Behaviors leading up to the foundation (19 to 35 months)
During this period, the child may: • Chew on a board book. (International Reading Association and the National Association for the Education of Young Children 1998, 198; 3–6 mos.; Parks 2004)	During this period, the child may: • Try to turn the pages of a paper book, turning several pages at one time. (scaled score of 10 for 9:16–10:15 mos.; Bayley 2006, 128) • Scribble with a crayon. (Scaled score of 10 for 12:16–13:15 mos.; Bayley 2006, 129) • Smile and point to or indicate pictures of favorite animals in a book. (10–14 mos.; Parks 2004) • Help the infant care teacher turn a page of a book. (14–15 mos.; Parks 2004) • Use an open hand to pat a picture while reading with a family member. (14–15 mos.; Parks 2004)	During this period, the child may: • Move behind the infant care teacher in order to look over her shoulder at the pictures, when there are several children crowded around. (18–24 mos.; Parks 2004, 68) • Turn the pages of a book one by one. (18–24 mos.; Parks 2004) • Listen as a family member reads short picture books aloud. (Scaled score of 10 for 21:15–22:16 mos.; Bayley 2006, 67; 27–30 mos.; Parks 2004) • Ask a question about a story; for example, "Bear go?" while turning from one page to the next. (24 mos.; Meisels and others 2003, 47)

References

Acredolo, L., and S. Goodwyn. 1988. "Symbolic Gesturing in Normal Infants," *Child Development*. 59: 450–66.

Acredolo, L., and S. Goodwyn. 1997. "Furthering our Understanding of What Humans Understand," *Human Development* 40: 25–31.

American Academy of Pediatrics. 2004. *Caring for Your Baby and Young Child: Birth to Age 5* (Fourth edition). Edited by S.P. Shelov and R.E. Hannemann. New York: Bantam Books.

Apfel, N. H., and S. Provence. 2001. *Manual for the Infant-Toddler and Family Instrument.* Baltimore, MD: Paul H. Brookes Publishing Co., Inc.

Bates, E.; L. Camaioni; and V. Volterra. 1975. "The Acquisition of Performatives Prior to Speech," *Merrill-Palmer Quarterly* 21: 205–26.

Bayley, N. 2006. *Bayley Scales of Infant and Toddler Development (Third edition).* San Antonio, TX: Harcourt Assessment Inc.

Bloom, L., and J. Capatides. 1987. "Expression of Affect and the Emergence of Language," *Child Development* 58: 1513–22.

Bloom, L., and others. 1996. "Early Conversations and Word Learning: Contributionsfrom Child and Adult," *Child Development* 67: 3154–75.

Bloom, L.; L. Rocissano; and L. Hood. 1976. "Adult-Child Discourse: Developmental Interaction Between Information Processing and Linguistic Knowledge," *Cognitive Psychology* 8: 521–52.

Carpenter, M.; K. Nagell; and M. Tomasello. 1998. "Social Cognition, Joint Attention,and Communicative Competence from 9 to 15 Months of Age," *Monographs of the Society for Research in Child Development,* Vol. 63, Serial No. 2554, 1–33.

Cheour, M., and others. 1998. "Development of Language-Specific Phoneme Representations in the Infant Brain," *Nature Neuroscience* 1: 351–53.

Committee on Integrating the Science of Early Childhood Development, National Research Council and Institute of Medicine. 2000. *From Neurons to Neighborhoods: The Science of Early Childhood Development.* Edited by J. P.Shonkoff and D. A. Phillips. Washington, DC: National Academy Press.

Cooper, R. P., and others. 1997. "The Development of Infants' Preference for Motherese," *Infant Behavior and Development* 20(4): 477–88.

Coplan, J. 1993. *Early Language Milestone Scale: Examiner's Manual* (Second edition). Austin, TX: Pro-ed.

Davies, D. 2004. *Child Development: A Practitioner's Guide.* New York: Guilford Press.

DeCasper, A., and W. Fifer. 1980. "On Human Bonding: Newborns Prefer Their Mothers' Voices," *Science*. 208: 1174–76.

Ehri, L., and J. Sweet. 1991. "Finger-Point Reading of Memorized Text: What Enables Beginners to Process the Print?" *Reading Research Quarterly* 26: 442–61.

Gogate, L., A. Walker-Andrews, and L. Bahrick. 2001. "The Intersensory Origins of Word Comprehension: An Ecological-Dynamic Systems View," *Developmental Science* 41 1–37.

Hart, B., and T. R. Risley. 1999. *The Social World of Children: Learning to Talk.* Baltimore, MD: Paul H. Brookes Publishing Co.

Hoff, E. 2005. *Language Development* (Third edition). Belmont, CA: Wadsworth/Thomson Learning.

Hulit, L. M., and M. R. Howard. 2006. *Born to Talk: An Introduction to Speech and Language Development.* New York: Pearson Education, Inc.

Ingram, D. 1999. "Phonological Acquisition" in *The Development of Language* (pp. 73–97). Edited by M. Barrett. East Sussex, U.K.: Psychology Press.

International Reading Association and the National Association for the Education of Young Children. "Learning to Read and Write: Developmentally Appropriate Practices for Young Children," *The Reading Teacher* 52(2) (1998): 193–216.

Jusczyk, J.; A. Cutler; and N. J. Redanz. 1993. "Infants' Preference for the Predominant Stress Patterns of English Words," *Child Development* 64: 675–87.

Kuczaj, S. 1999. "The World of Words: Thoughts on the Development of a Lexicon," in *The Development of Language* (pp. 133–59). Edited by M. Barrett. East Sussex, U.K.: Psychology Press.

Kuhl. P. K. 2000. "A New View of Language Acquisition," *Proceedings of the National Academy of Science of the United States* 97(22): 11850–57.

Kuhl, P. K. 2002. "Speech, Language and Developmental Change," in *Emerging Cognitive Abilities in Early Infancy* (pp. 111–33). Edited by F. Lacerda, C.

von Hofsten and M. Heiman. Mahwah, NJ: Lawrence Erlbaum Associates.

Kuhl, P. K. 2004. "Early Language Acquisition: Cracking the Speech Code," *Nature Reviews Neuroscience* 5: 831–43.

Lerner, C., and L. A. Ciervo. 2003. *Healthy Minds: Nurturing Children's Development from 0 to 36 Months.* Washington, DC: Zero to Three Press and American Academy of Pediatrics.

Locke, J. L. 1993. *The Child's Path to Spoken Language.* Cambridge, MA: Harvard University Press.

Meisels, S. J., and others. 2003. *The Ounce Scale: Standards for the Developmental Profiles (Birth-42 Months).* New York: Pearson Early Learning.

Moon, C., R. Cooper, and W. Fifer. 1993. "Two-Day-Olds Prefer Their Native Language," *Infant Behavior and Development* 16: 495–500.

National Research Council. 1999. *Starting Out Right: A Guide to Promoting Children's Reading Success.* Washington, DC: National Academies Press.

Pan, B., and C. Snow. 1999. "The Development of Conversational and Discourse Skills," in *The Development of Language* (pp. 229–49). Edited by M. Barrett. East Sussex, U.K.: Psychology Press.

Parks, S. 2004. *Inside HELP: Hawaii Early Learning Profile: Administration and Reference Manual.* Palo Alto, CA: VORT Corporation.

Plunkett, K., and G. Schafer. 1999. "Early Speech Perception and Word Learning," in *The Development of Language.* Edited by M. Barrett, 51–71. East Sussex, U.K. Psychology Press.

Rochat, P. J. Querido, and T. Striano. 1999. "Emerging Sensitivity to the Timing and Structure of Protoconversation in Early Infancy," *Developmental Psychology* 35(4): 950–57.

Schickedanz, J. A., and R. M. Casbergue. 2004. *Writing in Preschool: Learning to Orchestrate Meaning and Marks.* Newark, DE: International Reading Association.

Sulzby, E. 1985. "Children's Emergent Reading of Favorite Storybooks: A Developmental Study," *Reading Research Quarterly* 20: 458–81.

Whitehurst, G., and C. Lonigan. 1998. "Child Development and Emergent Literacy," *Child Development* 69(3): 848–72.

Appendix B

Reasons for Concern That Your Child or a Child in Your Care May Need Special Help

Children develop at different rates and in different ways. Differences in development may be related to personality, temperament, and/or experiences. Some children may also have health needs that affect their development.

This information may help to relieve or confirm any concerns you may have about a child's development.

The first five years are very important in a child's life. The sooner a concern is identified, the sooner a child and family can receive specialized services to support growth and development. Parents, family members, and caregivers may have concerns about a child's development and seek help when needed. It is always a good idea for families to discuss any questions they may have with the child's doctor. Caregivers should discuss concerns with families to see how best to support them.

Risk Factors

The following factors may place children at greater risk for health and developmental concerns:

Note: Copies of this brochure are available in English, Spanish, Vietnamese, Hmong, and Chinese. Ordering information is available at http://www.cde.ca.gov/re/pn/rc/orderinfo.asp or http://www.wested.org/cs/cpei/print/docs/221.

- Prematurity or low birth weight
- Vision or hearing difficulties
- Prenatal exposure or other types of exposure to drugs, alcohol, or tobacco
- Poor nutrition or difficulties eating (lacks nutritious foods, vitamins, proteins, or iron in diet)
- Exposure to lead-based paint (licking, eating, or sucking on lead-base painted doors, floors, furniture, toys, etc.)
- Environmental factors, such as abuse or neglect

Behaviors and Relationships

Some of the following behaviors may be cause for concern in any child regardless of age:
- Avoids being held, does not like being touched
- Resists being calmed, cannot be comforted
- Avoids or rarely makes eye contact with others
- By age four months, does not coo or smile when interacting with others
- By age one, does not play games such as peek-a-boo or pat-a-cake or wave bye-bye
- By age two, does not imitate parent or caregiver doing everyday things, such as washing dishes, cooking, or brushing teeth
- By age three, does not play with others
- Acts aggressively on a regular basis, hurts self or others

Hearing

- Has frequent earaches
- Has had many ear, nose, or throat infections
- Does not look where sounds or voices are coming from or react to loud noises
- Talks in a very loud or very low voice, or voice has an unusual sound
- Does not always respond when called from across a room even when it is for something that the child is usually interested in or likes
- Turns body so that the same ear is always turned toward a sound

Seeing

- Has reddened, watery eyes or crusty eyelids
- Rubs eyes frequently
- Closes one eye or tilts head when looking at an object
- Has difficulty following objects or looking at people when talked to
- Has difficulty focusing or making eye contact
- Usually holds books or objects very close to face or sits with face very close to television
- Has an eye or eyes that look crossed or turned, or eyes do notmove together

Moving

- Has stiff arms or legs
- Pushes away or arches back when held close or cuddled
- By age four months, does not hold head up
- By age six months, does not roll over
- By age one, does not sit up or creep using hands and knees, does not pick up small objects with finger and thumb
- By age two, does not walk alone, has difficulty holding large crayons and scribbling

- By age three, shows poor coordination and falls or stumbles a lot when running, has difficulty turning pages in a book
- By age four, has difficulty standing on one foot for a short time
- By age five, does not skip or hop on one foot, has difficulty drawing simple shapes

Communicating

- By age three months, does not coo or smile
- By age six months, does not babble to get attention
- By age one, does not respond differently to words such as "night night" or "ball"
- By age one, does not say words to name people or objects, such as "mama" or "bottle," or shake head "no"
- By age two, does not point to or name objects or people to express wants or needs
- By age two, does not use two-word phrases, such as "want juice" or "mama go"
- By age three, does not try to say familiar rhymes or songs
- By age three, cannot follow simple directions
- By age four, does not tell stories, whether real or make-believe, or ask questions
- By age four, does not talk so that adults outside the family can understand

Thinking

- By age one, has difficulty finding an object after seeing it hidden
- By age two, does not point to body parts when asked such questions as "Where's your nose?"

- By age three, does not play make-believe games
- By age three, does not understand ideas such as "more" or "one"
- By age four, does not answer simple questions, such as "What do you do when you are hungry?" or "What color is this?"
- By age five, does not understand the meaning of today, yesterday, or tomorrow

Concerns About a Child's Development

If you have concerns about your child's development, discuss them with your child's doctor. The doctor may recommend calling the local regional center or special education program at either the school district or the county office of education. The family may also contact these agencies directly. If you have concerns about a child in your care, discuss your concerns with the family. This brochure may assist you in talking with the family about specific concerns.

Next Steps

Once contact is made with a regional center or school district, a representative of the agency will provide additional information about services and,if appropriate, make arrangements to have the child assessed. The child may qualify for special services. Parents must give written permission for the child to be assessed and receive special education or early intervention services, which are confiden-tial and provided at no cost to the family. The family may also receive information about local Early Start Family Resource Centers and Family Empowerment Centers on Disability, which provide parent-to-parent support, resource materials, and other information.

Ages Birth to Three Years

Information on local resources regarding children birth to three years of age may be obtained from the following agency:

California Department of Developmental Services
P.O. Box 944202, Sacramento, CA 94244-2020
800-515-BABY (2229)
http://www.dds.ca.gov/earlystart
earlystart@dds.ca.gov

Ages Three to Five Years

Information on local resources regarding children three to five years of age may be obtained from the following organizations:

California Department of Education
Special Education Division
1430 N Street, Suite 2401
Sacramento, CA 95814
916-445-4613
http://www.cde.ca.gov/sp/se

California Childcare Health Program
1950 Addison Street, Suite 107
Berkeley, CA 94704
Child Care Hotline: 800-333-3212
http://www.ucsfchildcarehealth.org

Appendix C

The Responsive Process

Step One: Watch

Begin by just watching, not rushing to do things for the baby.

Watch for both verbal and nonverbal cues.

Step Two: Ask

Ask yourself: What messages is the child sending? What are the emotional, social, intellectual, and physical parts to the message? Does the child want something from me at this moment?

If so, ask the child: What is it that you want?

Step Three: Adapt

Adapt your actions according to what you believe to be the child's desires.

Watch how the child responds to your actions.

Modify your actions according to the child's response, and watch, ask, and adapt again.

Source: WestEd, The Program for Infant/Toddler Caregivers' *Trainer's Manual, Module I: Social-Emotional Growth and Socialization* (p. 40). Sacramento: California Department of Education.

ISBN 978-080111712-1

the **Program**
for
infant
toddler
care

Infant/Toddler Caregiving Nixon

A Guide to
Setting Up
Environments
Second Edition

Developed collaboratively by the
California Department of Education and WestEd
Sacramento, 2009

  WestEd